# FROM ROMULUS
# TO ROMULUS
# AUGUSTULUS

# LATIN FOR THE NEW MILLENNIUM
*Series Information*

### LEVEL ONE
*Student Text*
*Student Workbook*
*College Exercise Book, Levels 1 and 2*
*Teacher's Manual*
*Teacher's Manual for Student Workbook*

### ENRICHMENT TEXTS
*From Romulus to Romulus Augustulus:*
*Roman History for the New Millennium*
*The Original Dysfunctional Family:*
*Basic Classical Mythology for the New Millennium*

### LEVEL TWO
*Student Text*
*Student Workbook*
*Teacher's Manual*
*Teacher's Manual for Student Workbook*

### ENRICHMENT TEXTS
*From Rome to Reformation:*
*Early European History for the New Millennium*
*The Clay-footed SuperHeroes:*
*Mythology Tales for the New Millennium*

### LEVEL THREE
*Student Text*
*Teacher's Manual*

### ENRICHMENT TEXTS
*Latin 3: Select Latin Enrichment Readings*

---

### ELECTRONIC RESOURCES
www.lnm.bolchazy.com
www.bolchazy.com/ebooks.aspx
Quia Question Bank

# FROM ROMULUS
# TO ROMULUS
# AUGUSTULUS

# ROMAN HISTORY
## FOR THE NEW MILLENNIUM

**By Rose Williams**

Bolchazy-Carducci Publishers, Inc.
Mundelein, Illinois USA

*Editor:* Donald E. Sprague
*Cover Design & Typography:* Adam Phillip Velez
*Cover Illustration:* Detail from the Arch of Trajan, Rome
    © 2008 Jupiter Images Corp.

**From Romulus to Romulus Augustulus**
**Roman History for the New Millennium**

Rose Williams

**Bolchazy-Carducci Publishers, Inc.**
1570 Baskin Road
Mundelein, Illinois 60060
www.bolchazy.com

Printed in the United States of America
**2016**
by United Graphics

ISBN 978-0-86516-691-2

Library of Congress Cataloging-in-Publication Data

Williams, Rose, 1937-
    From Romulus to Romulus Augustulus : Roman history for the new millennium / by Rose Williams.
        p. cm.
    Includes bibliographical references.
    ISBN 978-0-86516-691-2 (pbk. : alk. paper) 1. Rome--History. 2. Rome--History--Chronology. I. Title.

DG77.W72 2008
937--dc22

                                                                            2008021649

*"beatos eos quibus datum est aut facere scribenda aut scribere legenda."*

"happy are those to whom it is given to do things worth being written or to write things worth being read"

– Pliny the Younger *Epistulae* 6.16

# TABLE OF CONTENTS

# FOREWORD

The early history of Rome is shrouded in legend, much of which we learn from the historian Livy. The stories cannot be taken as absolutely factual, as Livy often gives two versions of the same story, neither verifiable. But these stories represent Roman history as the Romans themselves accepted and revered it, and what people believe to be fact is often quite as influential as fact itself.

FOREWORD

# PREFACE

*From Romulus to Romulus Augustulus* is a brief survey of the history and literature of Classical Rome. A connected chronological overview of a people and their writings helps readers understand more about them, what they have done, and what they considered important enough to be written down for all time. How a people dealt with their environment both natural and social, as well as what trouble they got into and how they did or did not get out of it, is an integral part of language and literature study. As crises and triumphs flow one from the other, the people, the language, and the literature are carried along with them and shaped by them. This short reader will be useful for those studying ancient literature, language, culture, or history.

Terms that might be unfamiliar to the reader are emphasized in boldface type. The notes section at the back of the book provides an explanation for the terms.

*From Romulus to Romulus Augustulus: Roman History for the New Millennium* will serve as an enrichment and quick reference book for any group studying the ancient world. It is a good resource for those using the Bolchazy-Carducci textbook *Latin for the New Millennium* Level 1 and coordinates with it as follows.

## CORRELATION WITH *LATIN FOR THE NEW MILLENNIUM* LEVEL 1

II. Kingdom - 753–509 BCE (0–244 AUC)

    *LNM Chapters 1, 10, 11*

III. Early Republic - 509–265 BCE

    *LNM Chapter 4, Review 2, Chapter 12, Review 4*

IV. Middle Republic - 265–133 BCE

    *LNM Chapters 1, 2, 3*

# I. TIMELINE OVERVIEW

## 753–509 BCE (0–244 AUC)
### KINGDOM
### KINGS OF ROME

ca. 753–715 BCE Romulus founder and king of Rome

ca. 715–673 BCE Numa Pompilius, Sabine

ca. 673–642 BCE Tullius Hostilius, Latin

ca. 642–617 BCE Ancus Marcius, grandson of Numa Pompilius

ca. 616–578 BCE Lucius Tarquinius Priscus, Etruscan

ca. 578–534 BCE Servius Tullius, son-in-law of Tarquinius Priscus, possibly Latin

ca. 534–509 BCE Lucius Tarquinius Superbus, grandson of Tarquinius Priscus

## 509–27 BCE
### REPUBLIC
### A. 509–265 BCE EARLY REPUBLIC

509 BCE Annually elected magistrates

451–450 BCE Law of Twelve Tables written

390 BCE Rome sacked by the Gauls

367 BCE Consulship opened to plebs

312 BCE Censorship of Appius Claudius Caecus

298–290 BCE Third Samnite War

281–272 BCE War with King Pyrrhus

279 BCE Pyrrhic victory

## B. 265–133 BCE MIDDLE REPUBLIC

264–241 BCE First Punic War

218–20l BCE Second Punic War

196 BCE Flamininus proclaims freedom for Greece

184 BCE Censorship of Cato

149–146 BCE Third Punic War

133 BCE Murder of Tiberius Gracchus

## C. 133–27 BCE LATE REPUBLIC

112–106 BCE War with Jugurtha in Numidia

107–100 BCE Repeated consulships of Gaius Marius

82–79 BCE Sulla Dictator

73–71 BCE Revolt of Spartacus the Gladiator

63 BCE Consulship of Cicero

60 BCE First Triumvirate of Julius Caesar, Pompey the Great, and Crassus

59 BCE Consulship of Caesar

58–50 BCE Caesar's Gallic campaign

49–46 BCE Civil War between Caesar and the senatorial forces

46 BCE Suicide of Cato Uticensis

44 BCE Assassination of Caesar

43 BCE Second Triumvirate of Mark Antony, Octavian, and Lepidus

42 BCE Battle of Philippi

39 BCE Marriage of Octavian and Livia

31 BCE Battle of Actium

27 BCE Octavian given title of Augustus

# 27 BCE–476 CE
## EMPIRE
## A. 27 BCE –284 CE PRINCIPATE

27 BCE–14 CE Augustus Imperator

23 BCE Death of Marcellus

12 BCE Marriage of Tiberius and Julia

9 BCE Death of Drusus, Augustus' eldest stepson

4 CE Adoption of Tiberius by Augustus

14–7 CE Tiberius Imperator

19 CE Death of Germanicus

37–41 CE Caligula Imperator

41–54 CE Claudius Imperator

43 CE Conquest of Britain

54–68 CE Nero Imperator

54–59 CE Nero's "good years," guided by Seneca and Burrus

67 CE Vespasian's Judean campaign

68–69 CE Year of the Four Emperors

69–79 CE Vespasian Imperator

70 CE Capture of Jerusalem by Titus, son of Vespasian

79–81 CE Titus Imperator

80 CE Completion of the Coliseum, or Flavian Amphitheater

81–96 CE Domitian Imperator

96–98 CE Nerva Imperator

98–117 CE Trajan Imperator

117–138 CE Hadrian Imperator

138–161 CE Antoninus Pius Imperator

161–180 CE Marcus Aurelius Imperator

180–192 CE Commodus Imperator

193–211 CE Septimius Severus Imperator; establishes military dictatorship

211–284 CE Military unrest and political disorder; many emperors

## B. 284–476 CE DOMINATE

284–305 CE Diocletian becomes emperor and proclaims himself "Dominus"

293 CE Division of empire into Eastern and Western; four rulers

305 CE Abdication of Diocletian and Maximian

306–337 CE Constantine the Great Imperator

313 CE Edict of Milan, confirming religious toleration for Christians

324 CE Founding of Constantinople

325 CE Council of Nicaea

337–476 CE Varied emperors of varied abilities

410 CE Visigoths sack Rome

455 CE Vandals sack Rome

476 CE Romulus Augustulus deposed by Odoacer

# 476–526 CE
## REGES ITALIAE

476–493 CE Odoacer, Rex Italiae

493–526 CE Theodoric, Rex Italiae

# II. KINGDOM 753–509 BCE (0–244 AUC)

According to the Roman poet Vergil, the Trojan hero Aeneas, sailing west from Asia Minor after the Greeks destroyed Troy, was pursued by the anger of the goddess Juno and suffered many disastrous adventures. The one likely to prove most disastrous was a shipwreck which tossed him up on the shores of North Africa near Carthage, the city being built by Queen Dido, who had fled from the Phoenician city of Tyre after her brother Pygmalion had murdered her wealthy husband Sychaeus. With a bit of help from Aeneas' mother, the love goddess Venus, Dido fell madly in love with Aeneas. Encouraged by Juno, who hoped to circumvent the Fates' prediction that he would be the ancestor of a great people in Italy, Dido schemed to keep Aeneas in Carthage. Aeneas learned to care for the beautiful queen, but *pietas*, the greatest of Roman virtues, interfered. This demanding moral quality insisted on loyalty to the gods, who in this case had indicated that he should found his own city; loyalty to family, represented by his son, Ascanius, who would come to rule that city; and loyalty to country, in this case the new Troy he was to build. He was delaying happily in Carthage when the chief god Jupiter, spurred on by the complaints of Venus, sent Mercury the messenger god to demand that Aeneas remember his *pietas* and set sail for Italy at once.

Livy merely says that Aeneas was one of two Trojan leaders spared the penalties of war because they advocated the sensible policy of returning Helen, the wife of Spartan king Menelaus whom the Trojan prince Paris had stolen, and making peace. However that may have been, Aeneas came to Italy and founded the city of Lavinium, from which his son Ascanius set out to found the city of Alba Longa. (We use the word city in largely a poetical sense, as mud huts rather than great palaces were more likely to be the norm. Alba Longa probably had a hard time living up to its name of the Long White City.) After a number of generations Alba Longa was inherited by King Numitor, who had an ambitious brother named Amulius. After driving his brother out of the kingship, Amulius arranged an early death for his nephew. Numitor's male issue being no more, Amulius honored Numitor's daughter Rhea Silvia by making her a Vestal Virgin so that she could not marry. His planning was overset by the god Mars, however, and before Amulius realized that all, from his point of view, was not well, Rhea Silvia was the mother of twins, Romulus and Remus.

Amulius was a religious man. He knew the Furies, immortal female avengers who had snakes for hair and eyes that wept tears of blood, pursued those who killed relatives. He reasoned that if he put the boys in the flooding Tiber in a willow basket, however, and they happened to drown, he could not be blamed.

Romulus and Remus floated onto a sandbar and were found by a motherly wolf. In the best tradition of classical literature, the baby princes were discovered by a wandering shepherd. This shepherd, named Faustulus, took the boys home with him.

Romulus and Remus grew up in the hut of Faustulus. In their youth, when not herding sheep, they hunted game in the forest, where they encountered bands of robbers. The twins, developing an early Robin Hood spirit, robbed these robbers and distributed the spoils among

Children of the wolf.

their shepherd friends. The robbers, who like all really prosperous criminals could assume the guise of honest men, caught Romulus and his men in ambush and carried them off to be judged before Numitor, who was living in retirement on a portion of his lands given him by his generous usurper of a brother.

Faustulus, who had always had his suspicions about the disappearance of Rhea Silvia's twins and the she-wolf's sudden increase of family, told his story to Romulus and to Numitor. The result was a carefully plotted revolution that restored Numitor to the throne. Romulus and Remus then found that as a result of all their labors they were living in a kingdom whose absolute ruler was their grandfather. However kind and grateful he might be, a grandfather tends to restrict the activities of young men. So, in 753 BCE they set out in search of a place of their own.

The twins soon decided go back to their wolf-cave and found a city. This cave was on the Palatine, or Shepherds' Hill, which was an excellent strategic location, being one of an irregular ring of seven hills south of the Tiber River. Its desirability was enhanced because the fierce Etruscans lived north of the Tiber, and the river was given to flooding. Near the wolf-cave on the Palatine, Romulus and his men cut great square blocks of stone and began to lay foundations for the new city Romulus intended to rule. According to one story Remus, who wanted the city for himself, laughed at the budding fortifications and jumped over the low wall, and Romulus killed him. After that nobody laughed at Romulus' efforts, and when the city was named Rome after Romulus, nobody laughed at that, either.

Romulus and his men were proud of their new town, but it lacked one important element—women. Romulus and his men decided that settled homes, complete with wives, would be nice. But in setting out on their great adventure, they had neglected to bring along any females—perhaps the girls in Alba Longa, being more sensible than the males, refused to have any part of such an exploit. In any case, now that they had homes and property, more or less, the Romans dressed up and went over to court the daughters of the Sabines, who lived some three miles away. Their reception was definitely not encouraging. After a bit of constructive thought, the Romans set up an athletic contest and carried off the girls while their fathers were watching the games. The Sabines stormed back home and brought reinforcements to rescue the girls, of course, but after a lively battle and some intervention by the girls, who had been well-treated by their new Roman spouses, the two peoples settled down to live together and for a time were ruled by co-kings, Romulus and a Sabine with the alliterative name of Titus Tatius. Titus being short-lived, Romulus soon ruled alone with the advice of one hundred elders, called senators, whom he appointed. One day during a ceremony a thick cloud enveloped Romulus, and when the cloud dispersed his throne chair was empty. The people murmured that the senators standing nearby had done away with King Romulus, but the senators swore he had been carried away by the gods. Henceforth he was worshipped as the god Quirinus, and gave the senators much less trouble in the ether than he had on earth.

After Romulus came six more kings: Numa Pompilius, who established laws and religion; Tullus Hostilius, who, as his name implies, waged many a war; Ancus Marcius, who made the mistake of choosing an Etruscan named Tarquin Priscus to tutor his sons; Tarquin Priscus, who usurped the throne from his pupils; Servius Tullius, who married the king's daughter and was murdered by his son-in-law Tarquin Superbus, whose name means Tarquin the Arrogant. Tarquin Superbus, the last and nastiest of the Roman kings, lived up to his name with enthusiasm, killing and exiling many powerful people, including any senators whose property he desired or who he believed might be a threat to him.

As young Lucius Junius Brutus narrowly observed these gruesome proceedings, he decided his safety lay in stumbling around, saying stupid things, and generally behaving like a helpless soul. Biding his time, he waited for the proper moment to promote a change in government. His opportunity came in 509 BCE with the death of a true Roman heroine, Lucretia Collatinus. Sextus Tarquin, son of the king and heir to all his nastier traits, raped Lucretia, the wife of Tarquin Collatinus because she was not only beautiful but moral, and decency was one thing he could not stomach. Showing that Roman women as well as Roman men preferred death to dishonor, Lucretia, fully imbued with stern old Roman principles, called her father and her husband and told them, along with the rest of Rome, what had happened, and then plunged a dagger into her breast. Brutus, waving her death weapon, made a stirring speech calling the Romans to arms against the despicable Tarquins. The Romans, not even lingering to wonder how the dull and stupid Brutus had suddenly blossomed into orator and warrior, rallied to the cry and drove the king and his family out of Rome. So in 509 BCE, after the Roman Kingdom had lasted a little over two hundred years, the Romans began a remarkable experiment in self-government.

# III. EARLY REPUBLIC 509–265 BCE

In the power vacuum left by this startling turn of events, the *comitia centuriata*, a set of military census groups set up by King Servius Tullius, found themselves acting as voting groups. Having developed an understandable distaste for one-man rule, they elected two presiding officials, whom they called **consuls**, to serve for a single year. They then provided for a lively future by decreeing that each **consul** should serve as supreme commander of the military on alternate days.

Lucius Junius Brutus, now for his services called ***pater patriae*** and elected one of the first two consuls, set his new government on a careful watch for trouble, as nobody acquainted with the Tarquins expected them to take all this quietly. They did not disappoint the watchers, and, worse still, while they put together necessities for an attack on the infant republic, they received help from an unexpected quarter. Some privileged young Romans were discovering that life under an impartial law, especially when interpreted by strict constructionists such as Brutus and his counterpart, was more restricted than they had expected. Living under a despotic and licentious king, provided one took no part in politics, had certain advantages, and among those missing the grand old orgies and hoping to restore the king were Brutus' two sons. A slave told the whole king-restoration plot to Brutus who soon rounded up the suspects and found his sons among them. He did his duty as ***pater patriae***, although it deprived him of being the father of anything else. All the traitors were stripped, scourged, and beheaded. After this Brutus, almost with relief, went into the war the Tarquins finally mounted and died there.

Defeated in this attack, the Tarquins went seeking reinforcements among the Etruscans, their formidable relatives to the north. Lars Porsenna, king of Clusium and general overlord of Etruscans, was not averse to teaching these republic-loving upstarts a lesson and installing a friendly king in Rome. For the task he collected an army of 90,000, which considerably outnumbered the entire population of Rome. When surging southward with this massive crew, flattening fields and stirring up immense clouds of dust, he forgot that one of the main reasons Romulus built on the Palatine in the first place was that the Tiber River divided Etruria from Rome.

The Tiber was flooding wildly, and, as those clouds of dust in the northern sky became bigger and bigger, Horatius Cocles (whose *cognomen* means One-Eyed—he'd been to war before) decided that, if Rome was to survive, there was only one thing to do, even though his plan of action was likely to shorten his lifespan. He took up his position at the far end of the one narrow bridge that crossed the Tiber and told his friends to cut the bridge down behind him. As two heroic Romans ran out to help him, the Etruscans rolled up to the bridge's head and had a good laugh. Recovering from their mirth, they threw a great many spears, but the Romans deflected most of these with their shields and the rest ran afoul of the overhead timbers of the bridge.

While the Etruscans were deciding just who should charge those wicked Roman short swords, the bridge timbers cracked due to the enthusiastic efforts of the Romans on the opposite bank. Horatius' two friends ran back, but Horatius, pausing to put in a few last words about the Etruscans' family failings and probable ends, was too late. Therefore he jumped into the Tiber, armor and all, and was carried back to Rome on the swirling flood.

Porsenna was no fool, and he knew that the wildest river settles down after a while, so he waited for this inevitable happening and then laid siege to Rome. That is, he surrounded the city with his soldiers and waited for the Romans to starve. He thought it wouldn't be too long until they ate the last pigeons and rats and either surrendered or passed out of this world of tears to their questionable eternal reward.

Gaius Mucius was a young Roman with strong likes and dislikes: he disliked Etruscans in general and the diet they proposed to force upon the Romans in particular. So he asked the Roman Senate to let him go over to the Etruscan camp and kill the king. Whatever the senators thought of this project's chance of success, they didn't see too many alternatives, so they gave him their blessing and hoped he would succeed before the pigeons gave out.

Realizing that Porsenna had sentries everywhere, Mucius killed the first sentry he could sneak up on, donned his armor, and walked boldly into the camp. Here his next problem arose: he hadn't the faintest idea what the king looked like. He didn't like to ask; an Etruscan soldier should not be asking such things, particularly not with a Roman accent. He decided to use logic; seeing a huge silk tent in the middle of camp and a richly dressed individual in front of it paying the soldiers, he leaped forward and killed the payer. As any soldier could have told him, logic is seldom of much use in war. An even more richly dressed man stepped out of the tent and demanded, "Why have you killed my secretary?"

Mucius realized that this was no moment for lengthy explanations; he took advantage of the uproar arising among the soldiers who had not yet been paid. As he hacked wildly with his sword in every direction, a number of soldiers lost all interest in their pay, and indeed everything else, but Mucius was at last overcome and dragged before the king.

"Who are you?" demanded the king, who by this time was understandably a good deal annoyed. "My name is Gaius Mucius," was the reply. "I am a Roman citizen." This explanation was probably unnecessary, as Porsenna had most likely figured that out by now. "I wanted to kill my enemy," said Mucius, still giving in to his penchant for stating the obvious, "but I know how to die; a Roman can both give and endure pain. But know this: three hundred young Romans have sworn that they will neither eat nor drink till you are dead. The man who brings your food tomorrow may be your slave, or he may be a Roman."

Porsenna was a high-spirited warrior and a powerful king, and he did not take kindly to being threatened by his own prisoners in his own camp. "Bring a burning brazier," he howled, "and make him tell us everything!" Mucius thrust his right hand into the fire and watched it burn. "This," he said, "is what a Roman thinks of pain."

This stalwart behavior did not augur well for Porsenna's plan of action. After mulling it over a bit, Porsenna set Mucius free, not really knowing what else to do with him. The Romans welcomed the hero Mucius with great joy and some tangible rewards, one of which was a field across the Tiber that became known as the Mucian meadow. Mucius also received a new nickname, Scaevola, which means "Lefty," because he had lost his right hand. One wonders why he didn't have the good sense to put his left hand in the fire. But obviously he was a quick thinker, so perhaps he put his right hand into the fire because he was left-handed all along.

Considering that Horatius Cocles and Mucius might well be only samples of what Rome had to offer, Porsenna decided to discuss conditions of peace with the Romans. The obstreperous Tarquins demanded that one of the conditions of offering peace should be the restoration of the Tarquin kings. To the surprise of no one the Romans flatly refused that one, and Porsenna, who was gradually discovering that his Tarquin cousins did not improve on close acquaintance, did not insist but lifted the siege in exchange for the return of some lands taken from neighbors and some hostages.

One of the hostages was a maiden named Cloelia, who showed King Porsenna that all the audacity in Rome was not limited to the male sex. When the Etruscan camp was pitched near the bank of the Tiber, Cloelia led a band of girl hostages who leaped into the river and, undismayed by a hail of Etruscan arrows, swam across to Rome. Porsenna, furious, demanded that Cloelia the leader be returned to him, but, before his messengers had time to depart with his missive, admiration for the bold young woman overcame him. He tempered his message to read that, although for the arranged peace to hold the escaped hostage ring leader must be returned, he pledged that if she was restored to him he would send her home again unharmed. The Romans returned the girl, as the treaty required, and Porsenna praised her courage and told her that she might choose half the hostages and take them home with her. With a wisdom and discernment approved even by the hostages themselves, she chose the youngest of them, especially little boys, who were considered most open to injury. According to Livy Cloelia was rewarded, not with land as Mucius had been, but with an equestrian statue at the head of the Sacra Via in the middle of Rome.

After this adventure Porsenna decided that he had urgent business back in his capital of Clusium. He returned to his own kingdom, leaving his Tarquin cousins, whom he suddenly realized he had never really liked anyway, to their fate.

Rome now settled down (as much as any city in the middle of Italy in the fifth century BCE was likely to be allowed to settle down) and went about the business of becoming a republic, in which citizens are equal. As is usual in such cases, however, they soon discovered that some are more equal than others, as the patricians, descendants of outstanding founding fathers, claimed all the powerful posts. The plebeians, or common people, were allowed to man the armies, pay the taxes, and do anything else patricians didn't want to do. Wearying of this state of affairs, the plebeians noticed that they had only one advantage over the patricians: there were more of them. When the next skirmish flared up, the plebeians withdrew to a mountain a few miles away and left the Roman patricians to fend off their enemies for themselves. The patricians could see what was going to happen next, so, reluctantly they turned to a special kind of Roman hero, the first of a long line who would defend Rome not with his strong right arm, but with his persuasive tongue. They sent Menenius Agrippa to talk the plebeians back to town.

Agrippa told an affecting, if scarcely logical, story about a human body whose parts went on strike against the stomach because they all worked to feed it, while it did nothing but eat. Agrippa said that the hand, the mouth, the teeth, and the throat all made a pact to do nothing to feed the stomach, and as a result starved themselves. He said that the Senate was like a stomach which took in resources and relayed the benefits to all. This analogy might have had a few gaping holes, but plebeians were not trained in logic. They were impressed and agreed to come back to town, so the strength and unity of the new republic were preserved. Not slow to extract some benefits from a favorable situation, however, before their return the plebeians made the condition that they be allowed to elect officials of their own: this demand resulted in the creation of the office of Tribune of the People. These plebeian tribunes were legally protected from any physical harm and had the right to rescue any plebeian from the hands of a patrician magistrate. Later, the tribunes gained the even greater power of vetoing any act or proposal of any magistrate, including another tribune of the people.

One of the gaping holes in Agrippa's analogy was that the patricians were not all just stomachs; some of them were hands, etc. Many Roman patricians of the early days were small farmers, and we do mean small. Of course, since at this time there weren't many slaves, and a man often had to do all plowing and sowing either by his own strength or with the help of a reluctant mule, huge farms were largely impossible. About fifty years after the founding of the Roman Republic, Lucius Quinctius Cincinnatus, patrician though he was, was busily tending his four *jugera*, slightly less than three acres of land, when he was called upon to rescue his fatherland from a governmental (and monumental) foul-up. The two consuls for the year 458 BCE, Nautius and Minucius, had set out to deal with both the Sabines and the Aequi, two of Rome's usual assortment of enemies. While Nautius was destroying the Sabine fields, Minucius was supposed to take on the Aequi armies. Perhaps the assignments should have been reversed, since Minucius, once encamped in enemy territory, evidently lost whatever nerve he may have had and would not leave his camp. After the enemy had a chance to observe this interesting fact, they threw up earthworks around the camp and besieged it. Five horsemen, who evidently had more backbone than their commander, managed to break through and take the news to Rome.

The Romans had always suspected that the day might come when having two consuls, especially if they disagreed, could stymie things. They had provided, therefore, that in times of great emergency a special commander-in-chief, called a dictator, could be appointed to hold supreme power for a period of six months. They felt that Cincinnatus was the man for the job.

The messengers of the state arrived in the field where Cincinnatus, clad in a dusty work tunic and not looking in the least like a leading patrician, was right in the middle of spring plowing. After politely saying hello, and making a few remarks about the weather, they requested that Cincinnatus put on his toga. (Romans took great pride in these long, snow-white, cumbersome wraparounds, because they were the badge of Roman citizenship. But a Roman put on a toga only when he needed his dignity and was not about to do anything athletic, such as mounting a horse, or anything remotely resembling field work.) "Oh-oh," thought Cincinnatus, "this doesn't sound like good news." After he had cleaned up and was properly be-togaed, they hailed him as Dictator. Then they took him to a waiting boat and rowed him across the river to the city, where he collected soldiers, gave orders, made demands, and in general behaved like a dictator. Then he marched his recruits off to save Minucius, who was still sitting in his camp like a sardine in a can.

Not even pausing for breakfast after a night march, Cincinnatus' troops sounded the battle trumpet and attacked the surrounders of Minucius. Suddenly the Aequi found themselves the meat in a very nasty sandwich. Minucius' soldiers, hearing a Latin shout coming from outside the siege-works, raised a cry and charged forth. When the swords stopped clanging and the survivors were counted, Cincinnatus had a victory. He took the enemy camp, where his soldiers were delighted to find the makings of a really good breakfast.

After a quick triumphal parade and a few celebrations, Cincinnatus resigned the dictatorship and hurried back to his plowing. He had already spent sixteen days of the peak planting season on outside distractions.

Meanwhile the plebeians and their tribunes were trying to deal with the entrenched power structure. At least in the Bad Old Days of the Kings a plebeian accused of anything from murder to bad debt could appeal to the king. The founders of the republic had assured the people that they could appeal to the magistrates, but the magistrates changed every year, and the common people thought they would feel better if all the rules were written down in some nice, durable public form—like a few permanent tablets in the middle of the Forum. After much haggling and delay, in 452 BCE ten men, sensibly called the **decemvirs,** were appointed to write what turned out to be the Law of the Twelve Tables. Appius Claudius Decemvir, a member of the distinguished Claudii family who had immigrated to Rome from the land of the Sabines in the time of the kings, headed this commission, which enjoyed virtually unlimited authority. In the second year of his decemvirate Appius Claudius misused his authority in various ways, and, while the Twelve Tables were formally established in the Roman Forum in 449 BCE, he was disgraced and disappeared from history.

About fifty years later the Romans took on the Etruscans in their own territory. Nobody had expected this to be easy, and it wasn't. Marcus Furius Camillus, having been made Roman dictator, took due note of the fact that a ten-year siege of the great Etruscan city of Veii had produced little result, but he also discovered that the people of Veii believed that their city could never be conquered while there was water in Lake Albanus. Never one to balk at a little engineering challenge, Camillus had the lake drained and took the city from its suddenly demoralized defenders.

Moving on to the Etruscan city of Falerii, Camillus laid siege to it. Here he was approached by a schoolteacher as wily as he was unpleasant. This enterprising disgrace to education led his young charges, who just happened to be the sons of the city leaders, out of the city on a field trip that ended at the camp of Camillus. (Exactly why the parents allowed this questionable student activity remains a mystery). Brought before Camillus, the shameless teacher demanded gold for handing over these children whose parents would surely surrender the city to get them back. Camillus might like drainage projects, but he balked at using weapons such as this. Declaring angrily that the Army of the Roman People did not make war on children, he sent them back to their amazed parents, who surrendered the city. After all, why sit around snacking on withered vegetables and rats when a man of such high principles was your enemy? He seemed more than likely to offer generous surrender terms.

The Romans were very pleased with Camillus for his unusual ways of winning battles, as they spared both materials and men, but he soon fell out of favor. There was grumbling because he drove white horses, symbolic of the gods, in his triumphal parade. There was much louder grumbling because somebody suspected he had divided the loot unequally. Camillus found himself exiled from Rome.

The Romans couldn't have chosen a worse time to throw out a hero. When the Romans conquered the Etruscans, they removed a barrier between themselves and another less than pleasant force, the barbarian Gauls of far northern Italy. Around 390 BCE tribes of these Gauls, accustomed to fighting the Etruscans and rapidly growing bored, began to wage war on the Romans themselves in place of their flattened northern neighbors. These barbarians were truly worthy of the name, being big, untamed, and unwashed. In battle they had little discipline, but men of their size fighting like circle saws didn't seem to need it. At the river Allia they not only defeated the Romans, but sent them flying back into the city without even closing the gates. The Romans didn't stop running until they reached the citadel, a fortification on the Capitoline Hill. Here the Gauls promptly laid siege, and it appeared to all observers that Rome was finished. Camillus, swallowing his resentment, got the Romans out of this dismal situation by raising an army of neighbors and rushing to the rescue. The Rome Camillus rescued was in pretty bad shape after the Gallic siege, but he set to work so effectively that Livy called him *"parens patriae conditorque alter urbis"* that is, father of his country and second founder of the city. The achievements of Camillus grew greater and greater as years passed and stories were told. His novel notion of winning wars by honorable behavior made a lasting impression on later generations.

Rome was fortunate in her energetic and distinguished citizens, among whom was another member of the Appii Claudii family. This Appius Claudius was called Caecus "the blind," because when he was old the obvious happened to him. From 312 BCE to 285 BCE he served his country as censor, consul, and dictator. During and between these terms of office he built the Appian Way, the great road that leads from Rome to Capua, and the first aqueduct in Rome, the Aqua Appia. He extended voting privileges to common men and published the legal procedures and calendars which the priests had kept secret from the people. He retired from active life when he became blind, and only emerged when a major crisis arose.

The city shall have water.

Before we go on with the story of the Romans, we need to think about their environment. Few of us when in school are enthralled by geography, but perhaps we should be, as it often shapes the histories of nations. Part of Rome's climb to power was due to two geographical facts. The first is that Italy is basically a long mountain chain with a beach on each side. The second is that Rome, thanks to Romulus' selection of the seven hills just south of the Tiber River, lay a few miles from the river's western shore about halfway down the length of the peninsula. In the beginning she was only one of numerous small settlements dignified by the name of cities, but she was in fine position to deal with neighbors and enemies. Through conquest, colonization, and alliances, Rome slowly spread her power north and south along the peninsula.

Since Rome was content with control of high policy and allowed the cities under her power to run their own local affairs and squabble about them as much as they pleased short of war and mayhem, things went fairly smoothly. Roman taxes, while irksome, were usually not unbearable. The Romans, farmers to the core, opined, "You can shear a sheep every year; you can skin him only once." Since other great powers were much more addicted to the skinning process, Rome's allies usually stuck with her in murky situations and allies of the less far-sighted powers often joined the Romans if they saw a hope of forming new, more advantageous, alliances. This was a definite advantage for the Romans, as their success in gaining control over the Italian peninsula was rapidly exposing them to new enemies farther afield.

The city of Tarentum in south Italy mistreated Roman representatives and then called in Pyrrhus King of Epirus from Greece to help them in the war that promptly developed. This first extra-peninsular enemy of the Romans defeated them by the use of elephants in 280 BCE. Noting that all the Romans had died with wounds in front; i.e., none had fled, Pyrrhus was much impressed, and arranged a meeting to discuss returning such Roman prisoners as he had managed to salvage. The Roman hero Fabricius was sent to discuss the matter, and Pyrrhus soon learned that his attitude fitted right in with that of the Romans who had died on the battlefield. First he scorned Pyrrhus' gold and then he refused even to jump when Pyrrhus arranged for a concealed elephant to trumpet behind him. Pyrrhus had a sinking feeling that Fabricius was telling the truth when he said that he was impressed neither by bribes nor by threats. The king returned the prisoners gratis, as there really didn't seem to be much profit to be made from them.

Next Pyrrhus, hoping that Fabricius was one of a kind, or at least the last of those unimpressionable warriors, thought that perhaps Rome was now properly humbled and ready for peace. So he sent Cineas, his golden-tongued orator, to address the Roman Senate. The Senate listened to him, but while it was debating the matter, old Appius Claudius Caecus had himself carried into the Senate House and proceeded to give the first recorded political speech in Latin, which gives us the saying "every man is the architect of his own fortune"—a speech in which he said that if the senators did not see that Rome could and must fight off Pyrrhus, they were blinder than he was. The Senate sent Cineas back to Pyrrhus with some unpleasant evidence that Fabricius was not after all the last living stalwart Roman.

This Gaius Fabricius Luscinus, whom Pyrrhus had made such an unsuccessful attempt to scare, had moved to Rome from the Italian town of Aletrium (Livy *Ab Urbe Condita* 9.43). He had lost little time in becoming a leader; elected consul for 282 BCE, he had promptly defeated the Bruttians and Lucanians.

After the elephant incident Fabricius fought successfully against Pyrrhus later on, even sending a warning message to the king when his treacherous doctor came to Fabricius and offered to poison his employer, but it was left to Dentatus, in 275 BCE, to hand Pyrrhus a defeat that made him think well of finding better hunting grounds than Italy.

Discouraged by the indomitable Romans, Pyrrhus moved farther afield to Sicily. After making life merry for opposing armies in Sicily, in 272 BCE he went home for a parade and was killed by a rooftile thrown by a woman who evidently was not one of his admirers.

The Manius Curius Dentatus ("born with teeth" according to Pliny, *Naturales Historiae* 8.15) who so decisively defeated Pyrrhus was another small farmer. He was a plebeian, but very like the patrician Cincinnatus in many ways. Though consuls were usually elected from the patricians, Dentatus had been made consul in 290 BCE and, beginning a long career of making Rome's enemies wish they had picked on somebody else, had promptly put two of the worst, the Sabines and the Samnites, in their place. The Sabines were evidently a bit discouraged by this, but the Samnites, firmly believing that there are many ways to win, collected a large amount of gold and came to Dentatus while he was in his tiny hut cutting turnips into a pot for his evening meal. When they offered the treasure to Dentatus to change sides, or at least throw the contest, he called their attention to his being satisfied with his scanty dinner and stated a preference for controlling the people who had the gold rather than the shiny metal itself. Confronted by a talented soldier so totally blind to his best interests, what could they do but lose the contest? Dentatus defeated Rome's enemies time and again, and even found time to partially drain Lake Velinus and begin construction on Rome's second aqueduct, the Anio Vetus.

Pyrrhus had been the first extra-peninsular enemy the Romans had faced. He and his elephants had contributed significantly to Roman education, but, as the Romans extended their power to the southern tip of Italy, they met a set of much tougher teachers. The Carthaginians (called the Poeni by the Romans because they had come from Phoenicia), who lived in North Africa, controlled the island of Sicily, which was only eighteen miles from Italy. This was not to the Romans a desirable situation, and in 265 BCE they ventured for the first time outside their peninsula.

# IV. MIDDLE REPUBLIC 265 BCE–133 BCE

War with Carthage forced Rome to build a navy, with which, after several misstarts, they overcame the Carthaginians and invaded their homeland of Africa. Africa was at Rome's mercy until the Senate withdrew the main army and left a small force under Regulus, a commander as inflexible as he was brave. When the Carthaginians offered peace, he demanded a huge money payment, the islands of Sicily, Sardinia, and Corsica; and the surrender of the entire Carthaginian fleet. Infuriated, the Carthaginians put Xanthippus the Spartan in charge of their forces.

Xanthippus promptly reorganized the Punic army. He then defeated and captured Regulus, who had been so confident that he had not even secured a line of retreat. Sent home on condition that he would be free if he convinced Rome to make peace, Regulus insisted that Rome would win if she continued the war. His advice, which turned out to be good, was taken. Regulus returned to Carthage to be killed by the most unpleasant method Carthage could devise.

During the next few years while the Romans were trading insults with the Gauls who lived in northern Italy, Hamilcar of Carthage, who had become commander in Sicily near the end of the First Punic War, was plotting revenge on the Romans. He took his son-in-law and his three sons to Punic territories in Spain and built a power base there. The eldest of those sons, unfortunately for the Romans, was a precocious boy named Hannibal.

Rome's encounters with the Greek colonies in Southern Italy and with Carthage, coupled with her eventual defeat of that great Phoenician city, would not only establish her as a major world power but would also change her culturally and socially. Roman slaves were very often captives taken in war, and Lucius Livius Andronicus seems to have been one such captive. Probably born in the Greek colony of Tarentum and captured during the Roman war there, he became a slave to a Roman noble named Livius, perhaps M. Livius Salinator, the victor of Sena. Livius earned his living by private instruction in Latin and Greek, and when manumitted received the name of L. Livius Andronicus. His version of Homer's *Odyssey*, written in Latin Saturnian verse, became a staple of Roman schools. In 240 BCE, about a year after the end of the First Punic War, he produced the first of the many Greek plays he adapted to Latin. He composed and acted in the first comedy and the first tragedy in Latin, thus earning his reputation as the father of Roman drama. The fragments of his work which are extant are not numerous enough to allow us to form an opinion of his work, but it was definitely the beginning of a new cultural influence for Rome—the powerful thought and literature of Greece.

The next poet on the scene was Gnaeus Naevius (ca. 264–201 BCE), an Italian native who wrote historical plays, an epic, and comic plays. These retained some Greek settings, but they said far too much about good, and not so good, old Romans. Unfortunately some of his wittier remarks upset the Roman aristocrats, who could never take a joke on themselves, and he found himself imprisoned. After his release he made one too many clever remarks and fell afoul of the powerful Metelli clan; thus he lived the rest of his life in Utica in Africa.

Titus Maccius Plautus (254–184 BCE), a native Italian of evidently humble origins, saw all too clearly the troubles Naevius kept stirring up for himself. He confined his comic characters to Greece and saw to it that any Romans represented were properly disguised. He wrote some one hundred and thirty comedies (of which twenty still exist), which he carefully mentioned were adapted from Greek plays of the fourth and third centuries BCE written by such authors as Menander, Diphilus, and Philemon. Plautus' plays were called *fabulae palliatae*, or "stories wearing the Greek dress" after a type of Greek cloak, and even though they have a colorful Roman flavor and many references to Roman happenings, they did not bring retribution on the playwright's head. He enjoyed great success and a peaceful death.

Ennius (ca. 239–169 BCE), whose Roman historical works led many Romans to regard him as the Father of Latin Literature, was born about the time Livius Andronicus' first Greek plays were produced. Only bits of Ennius' work remain, but we know he wrote the *Annales*, an epic poem about the history of Rome, which was a staple of Roman education until the time of Vergil.

A slightly younger acquaintance of Ennius was the great Cato the Censor or Cato the Elder (234–149 BCE). As we have seen in the case of Appius Claudius Caecus, Roman writers were often more properly Romans Who Happened to Write, as they were likely to be politicians who had an axe to grind or a policy to defend. Cato was one of these, a true Roman patriot shaped by the cataclysmic events of the early second century BCE. During Cato's youth came the monumental struggle that would set Rome on its path to world domination. As we have said, after the First Punic War Hamilcar of Carthage took his son-in-law and his three sons to Punic (Carthaginian) territories in Spain and built a power base there. The eldest of those sons, a boy named Hannibal, carried on his father's vendetta with enthusiasm. In the summer of 218 BCE, knowing that the seafaring Carthaginians would be expected to attack by sea, Hannibal decided to march overland from Spain through the Pyrenees, then the Alps, and down into Italy. He seems to have thought that the Alps were just more hills, like the Atlas Mountains in North Africa. He soon learned his mistake. His army fared poorly in the Alps, but his war elephants fared even worse on those narrow cliff paths. In spite of his difficulties Hannibal defeated and slaughtered one Roman army after another, but he encountered two characteristics of the Romans which were so different from ordinary humanity that they ultimately defeated him. The first was the astounding fact that one could defeat the Romans, slaughter their men and utterly rout them, but nobody could make them realize that they were finished. Whenever she was defeated, Rome would raise another army from some source—allies, freed slaves, or Jupiter only knew what else—and come again.

The second odd aspect of the Roman psyche was the "shear 'em—don't skin 'em" philosophy. Hannibal was confidently expecting that as his victories mounted the Italian allies of Rome would join him. However, after taking a good look at their life under Rome, which wasn't too bad, and the habit the Carthaginians had of crucifying anyone who annoyed them, most of the allies stuck with Rome.

After Rome had endured a series of shattering military defeats at Hannibal's hands, old Quintus Fabius Maximus decided that the best way to deal with Hannibal was by not fighting him. Hannibal was far from home, and the Carthaginians tended to forget that their armies liked their little luxuries, like food, unbroken weapons, and whole uniforms. Ravaging the fields of Italy provided only poor sustenance for Hannibal's army, and Fabius saw to it that Carthage never got to win a battle, because he was never where Hannibal thought he would be at fighting time. This behavior earned Fabius the title of *Cunctator*, or Delayer, and made the high-spirited young Romans (the ones who weren't already dead, that is) think rather poorly of his courage, but it saved Rome.

After sixteen years of making life a perfect Hades for the Romans, Hannibal was called home to defend Africa because Publius Cornelius Scipio, soon to be nicknamed Africanus, had finally grown up and taken charge of things. From his youth this son of a whole line of Scipios had been a thorn in the Carthaginians' fleshy parts. Before he was seventeen he had saved his father (also Publius Cornelius Scipio) at the Battle of Ticinus. He had rallied the Roman troops (what was left of them) after their disastrous encounter with Hannibal at Cannae. While still very young he had gone to Spain as commander and, treading faithfully in the footsteps of Camillus and Fabricius, had decisively defeated the Carthaginians and impressed the Spaniards equally with his skill at war, his simple mode of living, and his chivalry when confronted with helpless captives.

Now Scipio had the good sense to invade Africa, and the Carthaginians at last felt compelled to call Hannibal back home—and fast. It didn't do any good, though; near Zama in North Africa Scipio defeated Hannibal in 202 BCE. For this Scipio received a magnificent triumph, but in true Scipionic fashion he paid for the games involved himself. He was given the **agnomen** Africanus, or conqueror of Africa, and became the hero of Rome. When the Romans proposed other honors, such as Consul and Dictator for life, he refused.

Old Fabius the Delayer was given the ancient ***corona obsidionalis***, which a Roman army had always presented to a general who lifted a siege or saved it from desperate peril. This signal honor, which boasted only about ten recipients in all of Roman history, was a plain grass wreath. The early Roman government was never inclined to be spendthrift.

After his service in the Second Punic War, Cato the Censor spent a long life living up to his title of censor with zest and gusto, even before he was elected to that office. One simple toga and plain bread were enough for him, and he didn't see what anybody wanted with more. As a military commander he was tough, fair, and thrifty; as a governor he traveled on foot with one slave; as a farmer he worked beside his slaves and ate what they ate. He said he despised both Greek and poetry, and he thought that the only way to give his son a decent education was to write the texts himself. Between his histories, speeches, and agriculture manuals, he certainly provided the boy with a thorough education. Of all these works only Cato's treatise on agriculture, *De re rustica*, survives in great part. It is the oldest extant literary work in Latin prose.

After the defeat of Hannibal, which broke Carthaginian power, King Philip V of Macedon, who was all too prone to confuse his abilities with those of his predecessor Alexander the Great, set out to add the city-states of Asia Minor to the ones he was controlling in Greece. Some of these city-states, being allies of Rome, demanded Roman help, which they received.

In 197 BCE Philip was conquered by Titus Quinctius Flamininus, who was very popular among the Greeks whom he had liberated until they discovered that he was neither going to kill off Philip, hopefully in a slow and grisly way, nor loot Philip's cities and divide the booty with them. The Roman Senate sent a panel of ten men to help Flamininus decide what to do with Greece, and he said it should be set free if Roman honor was to be upheld and Roman sanity was to be preserved—dealing with the excitable Greeks was hard on the Roman temperament.

The Greeks wept in joy and disbelief when they received their freedom, and set about using it to do in their fellow Greeks. Offering Flamininus any gift within their resources to show their gratitude, they were astounded when he asked only for the freedom of all Italian slaves in Greece. They dutifully rounded these up and handed them over, muttering to each other that no right-thinking man would ever understand a Roman. The ancient Samnites, who had had to watch Dentatus spurning their gold for a dinner of turnips, could have sympathized.

Scipio Africanus encouraged a philhellenic policy both during his consulship in 194 BCE and afterward, and Greek influence poured into Rome, transforming everything from art to education, much to the disgust of Cato and the conservatives. The Romans gained in refinement, but as Cato and others pointed out, some of the old virtues were being eroded. Cato's censorship of 184 BCE, while it scared the people it affected into some semblance of honesty and eroded the influence of the Scipiones, couldn't really change the trend. When Lucius Aemilius Paullus defeated Perseus, the king of Macedon, in 167 BCE, and allowed his sons to take only the king's books while the vast treasures of the king went into the public treasury, he was already out of step with the times.

During the bustling period after the Second Punic War, Marcus Pacuvius (ca. 220–130 BCE), a nephew of Ennius, wrote tragedies, as did his younger contemporary Lucius Accius (ca. 170–86 BCE). Both were highly regarded, but we have only fragments of their writings quoted by other authors.

The eldest son of Scipio Africanus, though he was precluded by ill health from both public office and full family life, adopted one of the sons of Lucius Aemilius Paulus, the conqueror of Macedon. This remarkable young man, now known as Scipio Aemilianus, became an outstanding warrior and a man of great learning. He sponsored the Scipionic Circle of learned men, which Cicero indicates included Polybius the Greek historian, Panaetius, a Stoic philosopher, and Lucilius, who originated the Roman genre of satire, as well as the outstanding playwright Terence. Scipio Aemilianus, according to Cicero and Polybius, practiced all the old Roman virtues. He was an outstanding orator and a generous and humane man. Ironically his name is most closely associated with the final destruction of Carthage.

Son of a whole line of Scipiones.

In the meantime Cato had never forgotten what he had observed in the Second Punic War, and he is famous for his often-repeated statement: *Carthago delenda est.* This phrase, meaning "Carthage must be destroyed," shows how much Cato and other Romans feared the resurgence of the Carthaginians. In 149 BCE Rome declared war on Carthage. The early part of this war went against the Romans, but Scipio Aemilianus as subordinate officer served his country well again and again, and in 147 BCE he was elected consul although he had not reached the legal age. After a year of desperate fighting and equally desperate heroism on the part of the defenders Scipio conquered Carthage, and, although he obeyed the Senate's order to destroy the city utterly, he salvaged and returned to Greece the art Carthage had taken from that country. When he returned to Rome, he received a splendid triumph and his full name was declared to be Publius Cornelius Scipio Aemilianus Africanus Minor.

During this period two poets of the Scipionic Circle, Lucilius and Terence, were establishing themselves for all time. Gaius Lucilius (ca. 180–103 BCE), born into the equestrian class of Romans, took the rude medley of writing which the Romans called **satura** and from it formed satire, that vigorous criticism of people and their actions which produced an indigenous Roman genre of literature owing very little to the Greeks. Although only fragments of his work remain, nevertheless, he enjoyed a great reputation in the Golden Age of Latin literature as is attested by the admiration and emulation Cicero and Horace held for him. Persius, Juvenal, and Quintilian show the admiration and emulation he commanded in the first century of the Roman Empire. To his example and influence we owe the great satires of Horace, Juvenal, and Persius, which established for the literary world a new genre.

Publius Terentius Afer (ca. 195–159 BCE) was brought to Rome as a slave by Terentius Lucanus, a Roman senator. He was manumitted and took the name Terentius from his former master and Afer from Africa, the place of his birth. He wrote six Latin comedies, the *Andria, Hecyra, Heautontimoroumenos, Eunuchus, Phormio,* and the *Adelphi,* basing his work on that of the Greek comic playwrights, especially Menander. The first of these works, staged in 166 BCE, attracted the attention of educated Romans, and his talents led to his being received into the Scipionic Circle. He evidently died at a fairly young age either in Greece, where he had gone to study literature, or shortly after he returned to Rome. His six plays are either fairly close adaptations of Menander or a mixture of various Greek plays. However, he chose plays which deal with universal human problems to restructure into Latin literature; thus they speak to all eras. The grace and beauty of their Latin is Terence's own.

Scipio Aemilianus continued to serve his country. He had voluntarily gone to Spain in 151 BCE and calmed the restless natives there. After the Third Punic War his influence was enhanced. When he was elected censor in 142 BCE, he was quite as assiduous as Cato had been in checking luxury and immorality, though hampered by a less than enthusiastic colleague. Having been elected consul again in 134 BCE, he subdued the city of Numantia and brought the province of Hither Spain under firm Roman control. For his services he received the additional **agnomen** of "Numantinus."

Meanwhile a crisis was developing. While Rome's culture was being enriched by contact with the older Mediterranean civilizations she had encountered and largely conquered, her civil government was falling into grave difficulties. The continuous wars of the second century BCE had kept Roman soldiers away from their small lands for years on end, and these had been neglected and finally absorbed into large **latifundia** controlled by the wealthy. When the soldiers returned home at last, they had nowhere to go, and swelled the unemployed masses which thronged in the city of Rome. Thus the hungry mobs grew, while the number of men with enough financial assets to serve in the Roman military shrank. Tiberius Sempronius Gracchus, who had been elected Tribune of the People in 133 BCE, proposed the *lex Sempronia agraria,* a set of land reform laws basically requiring the government to enforce the statutory but long ignored limit of 500 *iugera* of public land per person, to confiscate the remaining public land, and to distribute it to the displaced veterans. The conservatives in the Senate, many of whom controlled and used the land in question, were unlikely to pass such reforms, so Tiberius bypassed the Senate and went directly to the *Concilium Plebis*, the Popular Assembly which only a tribune could convene and which enthusiastically supported him. When Tiberius sought re-election for 132 BCE, a riot broke out. Tiberius was assassinated in the Roman Forum and the rule of law in Rome received a serious blow. Thus the death of Tiberius Gracchus is considered the end of the Middle Republic. A new era of Roman fighting against Roman had begun.

The army made Rome great.

# V. LATE REPUBLIC 133–27 BCE

Rome was fast being divided into two political parties, the *Optimates*, which was composed of the patricians and the upper classes, and the *Populares*, or common people. Scipio Aemilianus favored moderation, and thus did not approve either of the staunch conservativism of the Senate or of the extreme liberal policies of his brother-in law Tiberius Gracchus. When Gracchus was assassinated in 133 BCE, Scipio made no secret of his belief that the young man had been justly slain for treason. Scipio thus incurred the bitter hatred of the *Populares*, and when he was found dead in his bed in 129 BCE on the day on which he had intended to make a speech concerning the agrarian policies of Tiberius Gracchus, many people suspected what later on Cicero openly said, that Scipio had been slain by the conservatives, who liked his moderation no more than the liberals did.

Tiberius Gracchus' younger brother Gaius was elected Tribune of the People in 123 and 122 BCE. Through the Popular Assembly he enacted laws aimed at punishing his brother's murderers, relieving the poor, and weakening the power of the Senate, but when he tried to extend the relief he gave to the Roman masses to all Italians, the Roman commons decided he had gone too far, and he and his supporters were massacred in a riot on the Aventine Hill in the heart of Rome.

The reforms of the Gracchi brothers, however well-intentioned they might have been, shredded the traditional powers of the Senate and people and added to the general social upheaval and the erosion of the Roman governing system. Their violent deaths were the first of many soon to come, as unscrupulous politicians exploited the weakened system. The situation was not improved by the fact that the soldiers in the victorious armies returning from conquest had reason to stay with their commanders, as there was little for them in the civilian world. To make matters worse, those commanders were conspicuously lacking the unselfish mettle of Aemilius Paullus, Cato Censor, and the two Scipiones.

Shortly after the death of the Gracchi, Gaius Marius, an ambitious young Roman of probable equestrian rank, impressed one of the great Metelli clan so much that he was taken to Africa as senior legionary commander. After undermining Metellus and getting his command, he conquered the armies of the wily Numidian king, Jugurtha, but made the mistake of parading Jugurtha through Rome as his prisoner when the Numidian king had actually been captured by Lucius Cornelius Sulla, a young patrician whose family had been undistinguished for many years. From this point on relations between these two ambitious climbers went from bad to worse, with Marius claiming the loyalty of the *Populares* and Sulla that of the *Optimates*. For the next sixteen years or so they raised and trained their own armies, defending Rome and expanding her power between bouts of slaughtering each other's adherents.

Marius was almost twenty years older than Sulla, and one would have thought old age and exhaustion would have removed him from the contest, but he was made of hardy stuff. In 88 BCE Sulla's forces got the upper hand and Marius was declared a public enemy; Marius, however, escaped to Africa to continue helping Sulla create disaster. By the time Marius died in 86 BCE, the civil power was in shambles and half the populace either dead, exiled, or impoverished. Having used his army to destroy a few leftover rivals from the Marian camp such as Sulpicius and Cinna, Sulla in 81 BCE became dictator, and now, unhindered by Marians, he was able to wield complete power.

Sulla could be generous with his adherents, but he had given ample proof of how dangerous he could be when crossed. However, two Romans who would shape the classical world refused, even though very young, to pander to him. Gaius Julius Caesar flatly refused to divorce his wife at Sulla's command. Not only had Caesar married Cornelia, the daughter of the consul Cinna whom Sulla had killed, but he also had an aunt who had married Marius. After young Caesar stated his firm intention of remaining in his present marital status, he wisely went East, where he remained until Sulla's death.

In Italy, at this time, Chrysogonus, a freedman who was one of Sulla's more outrageous boon companions, conspired with poor relations of the victim to have Sextus Roscius, a very wealthy man, murdered. He then listed Roscius among Sulla's proscribed "traitors" so that his property could be confiscated. The poor relations and Chrysogonus were so greedy that they went too far—they accused the dead man's son of his murder. Young Marcus Tullius Cicero, who was making quite a name for himself as a legal advocate, defended young Roscius so well that he won an acquittal and the whole plot was exposed. Cicero wisely took the position that Sulla was unaware of these dastardly deeds, but after young Roscius was acquitted Cicero felt it was best to go to Greece for extended studies.

Sulla's abdication after two years of power and his subsequent death left Rome in yet another uproar, for Sulla had left his power to the Senate, which was not the "assembly of kings" that Cineas extolled. They were not prepared to deal with the citizens who wanted their rights back, the pirates on the sea, the gangs of runaway slaves on land who roamed and robbed, or the escaped gladiator Spartacus who was perched on the volcano Mount Vesuvius, of all places, with a huge slave army, and soon marched forth to defeat armies and plunder the countryside. Marcus Crassus and Gnaeus Pompey between them finally sent Spartacus and his army to their grisly rewards. Crassus actually defeated them, but Pompey decorated Roman roads with their crucified bodies and claimed the victory. This gave Crassus a life-long grudge against Pompey which surfaced every once in a while, much to the delight of the Senate. That august body, which had never recovered from its fear of kings and always shuddered when confronted by a man of outstanding ability, reluctantly gave Pompey power over the seas. Having destroyed the pirates, he went to Asia Minor to defeat King Mithridates VI of Pontus. Matters were stabilized for the moment, but the tensions beneath the surface were bubbling briskly.

While Pompey was strengthening his right to power in the East by military victories, Caesar, Crassus, and Cicero were making their mark back in Rome. Crassus had not only his defeat of Spartacus but also his immense wealth to throw on the scale. Caesar had his relationship to Marius, his ancient lineage, and his own great ingenuity, which had scarcely begun to surface yet. Cicero had his unmatched speaking ability.

Partly because the freed slave Tiro so painstakingly preserved and published over eight hundred of Cicero's letters, we know more about his private life and personal feelings than about any other ancient figure. Throughout his life Cicero showed some interesting shades of character. His defense of young Roscius was only the first of the instances in which he risked the enmity of the powerful for a great cause, usually the defense of his beloved country. Yet he was almost childish in his demands for recognition and invariably blind to the glaring faults of the senatorial class, which he finally, after being elected consul, was allowed to join. It is always surprising to discover this thoroughly human personality behind a facility with language so great that he virtually recreated Latin, folding into it more dynamic, more exact, and more effective expression.

Cicero's oratorical powers were badly needed during his consulship in 63 BCE, as the Roman historian Gaius Sallustius Crispus shows in his historical account of the Catilinarian Conspiracy. Lucius Sergius Catilina, who was Cicero's senior by about two years, had sprung from an old patrician family which had lost most of its influence, the bulk of its wealth, and all of its honor, if it had ever had any. He had been one of Sulla's least pleasant young friends and, having found his prospects drying up after Sulla's demise, set out by means fair or foul to climb through the *cursus honorum.* Some offices he did obtain, but the consulship eluded him, and he developed a plot to kill Cicero and his fellow consul and seize control by insurrection. Cicero exposed this plot in a series of brilliant speeches and saved the state, a fact which he never allowed anyone to forget. Because they were very powerful and very dangerous, as consul Cicero brought a motion before the Senate to execute quickly without the trial required by law five captured Catalinarian conspirators against whom there was overwhelming written evidence. The Senate voted for this, but later through the machinations of a clever enemy, Publius Clodius Pulcher, Cicero was exiled from Rome because of this execution.

Cicero's stormy public life inevitably took its toll on his private life. In one touching letter written from exile to his wife Terentia he sends his love to her, his son Marcus, and his daughter Tullia, and regrets that he has brought suffering on them through his political activities. His regret is sharpened because he says he depended for support on people who let him down and did not follow those who wanted to help him. There may be some momentary weakness here, but there is also a courageous determination to face his own missteps.

One of those who always wanted to help Cicero was Julius Caesar, but Cicero held aloof from Caesar's offers of position and power, always fearing what Caesar might do to the country. Cicero never lost his admiration of the Senate as it had been, not as it was in his day, and he was firmly convinced it was capable of ruling wisely and justly. Caesar, who understood the Senate's weaknesses and had few illusions about himself or anybody else, did just what Cicero had feared he would do; he became permanent dictator. This development and the death of his beloved daughter Tullia struck Cicero as a double tragedy. He had given his very deepest love to two objects—the Roman Republic and his daughter Tullia, and now he had lost them both. Cicero said that he must now learn how to live a quiet life under the absolute domination of a man who was wise, liberal, and very fond of him, but who maintained a complete control over everything, a situation which was galling to the republican Roman spirit. He then proceeded to devote his energy to writing and to bringing many philosophical ideas into Latin and to reshaping the language into an apt expression for them.

Julius Caesar had not come quickly or easily to this supreme power. Born in 100 BCE, six years after Cicero, he had withstood Sulla's demands as a very young man and then lived fairly quietly during his young manhood. He was elected *Pontifex Maximus* in 73 BCE and slowly rose through the *cursus honorum*. As **propraetor** of the province of Further Spain Caesar proved he could win both battles and the affection of soldiers and provincials, not to mention that of the common people. During his year as consul he ratified Pompey's treaties with the Near East countries, made a strict law limiting the supplies that Roman governors could demand from the hapless provincials, and forced the publication of senatorial transactions. Only when Caesar was made proconsul of Cisalpine Gaul and Illyria after his consulship, however, did his military brilliance come into full view. He conquered numerous peoples and came into contact with still others, observing and often recording their life-styles, beliefs and habits in his precise and masterly work *De bello Gallico*. During his nine years in Gaul he added to the Roman Empire an area almost one third of its size. Thanks to his largely tolerant policies, this area was loyal, not to Rome, but to Caesar. His advance toward Rome at the head of one legion despite the Senate's order to disband his entire army precipitated the Civil War Pompey led against him, which Caesar records in *De bello civili*. It was rumored that he intended these lean, spare accounts as notes for some historian to use, but it was also rumored that they were so well written that no historian cared to try to improve them. The Civil War ended with Caesar's establishment as dictator.

In July 46 BCE, Caesar, returned to Rome and undertook many reforms, including an overhaul of the calendar, which certainly needed some help. Less than a year later he had to go to Spain and subdue Pompey's son, who made his father look like a saint—even the most anti-Caesar politico shuddered at the thought of Young Pompey. Finally in September 45 BCE, Caesar settled down to deal with such mundane affairs as overwhelming debt, bloated welfare rolls, footloose soldiers, and malarial marshes. His governing was excellent, but unacceptable to the senators who

Men believe what they want to believe.

still feared one-man rule and longed for their old power. March 15, 44 BCE, a group of senators approached Caesar on his way to the senatorial meeting with a false petition and stabbed him to death.

Rome was stupefied by Caesar's murder, but it did not remain that way very long. It soon made its anger perfectly plain to the conspirators who had assassinated Caesar. This bewildered the conspirators, who had expected to be thanked for killing the man who was stabilizing Rome and for returning things to the bloody state of chaos that had existed before him. They fled to the Capitol, and could not be tempted out of it for the Senate meeting that Mark Antony, as consul and now ranking officer, set up. This complicated Roman owed his continued existence to the high-minded Brutus, who thought sinking a sword into his lifelong friend and mentor (and according to the more gossipy traditions, his possible father) was a pious act of service to the gods, but that to add the blood of the debauched and unpredictable Antony might make the whole thing look like murder.

The Roman Senate met only to face a difficult dilemma. They hated to condemn the conspirators, who were their colleagues and who had their sneaking sympathy, as murderers. If they hailed them as deliverers, however, they had a raging mob of Romans just outside the Senate House to deal with, and Antony hastened to remind them that such a hailing would render Caesar accursed and all his acts by which everyone had benefited null and void. Some of those whom Caesar had helped would not even be senators any more; many would lose their offices. Furthermore, Octavian, Caesar's great-nephew and adopted heir, was becoming the center of an army of Caesar's devoted and war-tested veterans.

Cicero invoked the Athenian policy of proclaiming a "forgetting"; this meant that both sides agreed to forget the recent past and take no vengeance for it. That satisfied the Senate, which was soon to learn that the ordinary Roman had little patience with such political refinements. The people's anger was red-hot, and the public funeral oration the Senate allowed Antony to give for Caesar stoked this fire which needed no stoking. Antony reminded the people of all Caesar's mighty deeds and capped this moving speech by reading Caesar's will, in which he had left to each Roman from his fortune a monetary gift equaling several weeks' wages. That did it. The conspirators and their followers fled to Greece.

Octavian won enough popular, military, and senatorial support to be appointed consul of Rome at the age of nineteen. He negotiated a five-year alliance with Antony and Marcus Lepidus, and these three formed a new triumvirate which would punish Caesar's assassins and then divide up the Roman world. The conspirators, led by Brutus and Cassius, were defeated and killed at the Battle of Philippi in 42 BCE.

Cicero survived Caesar by about eighteen months. With the government once again in flux after the assassination of Caesar, Cicero stepped forward to lead the fight against the growing power of Mark Antony. His words to Antony in the **Second Philippic** are eerily prophetic: "I defended the Republic as a young man; I shall not desert her now that I am old; I despised the swords of Catiline, I shall not fear yours. I would offer this body gladly, if in dying I might leave the Roman people free." The irony is that this brave but foolhardy statement and the gruesome death it brought on him ultimately helped to free the country from Antony's power, but neither this nor anything else could salvage the Roman Republic. Octavian, great-nephew and heir of Julius Caesar, had already begun the arduous ascent to become Augustus, first Emperor of Rome.

Cicero and Caesar were arguably the finest prose writers of the first century BCE, but a young acquaintance of theirs would be its superb lyric voice. Tennyson calls Gaius Valerius Catullus "the tenderest of Roman poets" (*Frater, Ave Atque Vale*). He was certainly the most Romantic, not only because he was a distracted lover but also because his brief, tempestuous life and early death are the very stuff of which Romance is made. According to scholars' best calculations he lived just about thirty years (ca. 84 BCE–54 BCE). He is represented today by only 116 poems, many of which have only two or four lines. In spite of this short life and sparse output, he is one of the most influential writers of Roman literature, and possibly the only Roman to die, through a combination of malnutrition and illness, for love.

Much Greek and Roman literature has been lost; scholars estimate that we have less than ten per cent of the writings that we know existed in classical antiquity because many of the lost works are quoted or at least mentioned in the works we do have. Among the lost works are many written by Catullus' friend Cornelius Nepos (ca. 100–25 BCE), a Roman biographer and historian whose life spanned the difficult transition from Republic to Empire. He is said to have been born in Hostilia, a village in Northern Italy not far from Verona, and, from the friendships he made, he must have spent a good deal of time in Rome. He was evidently a friend both of Catullus and of Cicero, but little is known of him except for many references to him and passages from his works found in other writers. Aulus Gellius (*Noctes Atticae* 15.28) corrects an error in his *De vita Ciceronis*. Only fragments of Nepos' *De viris illustribus* remain, including an anecdote of Cato given by Gellius (*Noctes Atticae* 9.8). Some twenty-three sections of his *Liber de excellentibus ducibus exterarum gentium* including the stories of Themistocles, Miltiades, Epaminondas, Pausanias, Hannibal, Hamilcar, and Datames the Persian are extant. These biographical sketches praise their subjects and stress a moral point, but they do not plunge deeply into historical events or human character. The short biography of the elder Cato and a longer one of Cicero's friend Atticus, excerpts remaining from his *Liber de Latinis Historicis*, adopt a wider and more realistic approach. It is ironically probable that his only fully surviving work is the *Excellentium Imperatorum Vitae*, which appeared in the reign of Theodosius I as the work of Aemilius Probus. Subsequent scholarship has shown that Probus actually edited and abridged the book, which seems to have been originally a work of Nepos.

# VI. A. PRINCIPATE ERA OF THE EMPIRE
## 27 BCE −284 CE

Both the Roman Senate and the great warriors of Rome underestimated young Octavian. After he had joined Antony to defeat the assassins of Caesar, he overcame Antony and all other contenders for major power, and gradually brought order and stability to the shattered Roman world. In 27 BCE the Roman Senate granted Octavian the name **Augustus**. Almost with a sigh of relief the Senate also gave him the legal power to rule Rome's religious, civil, and military affairs, and itself became an advisory body, effectively making him Emperor. To his efficiency in all things large and small he added great modesty and a careful observation of Republic formalities. Though he had been given the title **Augustus** and was for his victories called **Imperator**, he preferred the title of **Princeps**, or First Citizen, and insisted that consuls be elected every year, although he was always chosen and effectively named the other one. All this kept resistance to his rule to a manageable minimum. He set about restoring Rome psychologically as well as physically, and enlisted in this effort his wealthy friend Maecenas, who became the patron of a circle of artists commissioned to restore the sense of dignity, ethics, and religion to a people demoralized by one hundred years of civil unrest and war.

Maecenas was that very rarest among human beings—a man of wealth and a man of letters, devoid of personal ambition and devoted to his country. Both Maecenas and Augustus were fortunate in that within the usual crowd of needy poets lurked Vergil, Horace, and Propertius. All three of these men had become at least somewhat needy through the massive confiscations of property which took place while Augustus was rewarding his victorious veterans. Horace had even fought briefly for Brutus, who was a leader among the conspirators who had slain Caesar, but he says himself that he was the world's worst soldier, hiding under a bush at the first sign of disaster. Possibly Augustus thought that Horace had been of more use to him in the opposing army than in his own. Certainly he held no grudges for the past; soon Horace was pardoned and became a member of the circle of Maecenas, to which the generous, unworldly Vergil, totally lacking in professional jealousy, had introduced him. Maecenas, realizing that Horace was ill-suited to imperial court life, provided the poet with a small farm in the hilly Sabine country beyond Tibur (Tivoli). There Horace, freed from the daily chore of earning his bread the hard way, devoted himself to writing. His literary production was quite varied, including the *Epodes*, four books of Odes (*Carmina*), and the *Epistulae*. His brilliance shines in several poetic genres, but it is especially memorable as he builds upon the foundation laid by Lucilius to become the creator of the gentle and humorous Horatian satire which glows in his *Sermones*.

Propertius had grace and wit, but was not overflowing with Good Old Roman Patriotism. He was very little help in rebuilding Rome, preferring to rebuild over and over again his relationship with a Jezebel he called Cynthia.

Vergil, however, was the crown jewel of Maecenas' brilliant circle. Perhaps because of the talent shown in his *Eclogues* and *Georgics*, this shy and quiet man was assigned the task of writing a national epic to restore the self-esteem and patriotic fervor of Rome. Taking the trials of Aeneas as his text, he succeeded so well that he, like Byron, "awoke to find himself famous." He did not take to notoriety nearly so well as Byron did, and sometimes fled from his fans and hid in the nearest house. His dying wish was that the *Aeneid* should be destroyed because he had not perfected it. Augustus, perhaps feeling that he needed great literature much more than he needed to be fussy about Vergil's personal preferences, ordered it published instead. Scholars through the ages have had a wonderful time discovering the parts of the *Aeneid* that need polishing, but it remains one of the world's greatest literary works.

Forty-five year rule established Pax Romana.

Maecenas and Augustus did not confine their support to poets. Another member of Maecenas' charmed circle was the historian Livy, who in 142 books set forth Everything That Had Ever Happened in Rome. From the thirty-five or so of these books which now exist, we can see that Livy highlighted in his historical anecdotes the sterling qualities, bravery, and patriotism of the early Romans. As was mentioned in the Preface to this book, Livy often gives two versions of the same story, neither verifiable. Whether the stories are literally true or not, they illuminate and underscore Roman values.

The peace and economic stability which Augustus' **Pax Augusta,** later to expand into the **Pax Romana,** brought to Rome gave the Romans a respite which they needed and a chance to expand their heedless leisure which they did not need. Poet-in-chief of the new pleasure-seekers was Publius Ovidius Naso (43 BCE–17 CE), who grew up during Octavian's difficult rise to power, and as an adult enjoyed the Pax Augusta that the Imperator had created a little too much. His excellent, witty, and very popular verse was sometimes seriously at odds with Augustus' drive to restore morality, and for reasons never made entirely clear in 8 CE he was exiled, or rather relegated, to little Tomi on the Black Sea, where he stayed for the rest of his life.

Augustus Caesar achieved an almost incredible feat in his reshaping of the debilitated Roman Republic into the dynamic Roman Empire, but both his *fortuna* and his outstanding acumen in dealing with people seemed to desert him in the area of personal life. Some years earlier, in a startling departure from his usual sober behavior, he had forced Tiberius Claudius Nero to divorce his pregnant wife Livia because Augustus himself wanted to marry her. This romantic escapade set off a chain of events worthy of a Greek tragedy, as Livia had a young son by Claudius and was soon to bear another son. This second boy was widely rumored to belong to Augustus, although Tiberius Claudius claimed him. In an ordinary family such things could lead to a nasty amount of sibling rivalry; in the family of an empire ruler, the results were cataclysmic and long-lasting. Augustus settled down with Livia to a simple life of living cleanly, governing wisely, and avoiding extravagance, which behavior may explain the lack of films set in this historical period. His very clothes were woven by the women of his family. His daughter Julia, however, the product of Augustus' earlier marriage to Scribonia, reportedly preferred the way of life Augustus was trying to stamp out to the one he was trying to establish.

Woman is a political pawn.

## JULIO-CLAUDIAN EMPERORS

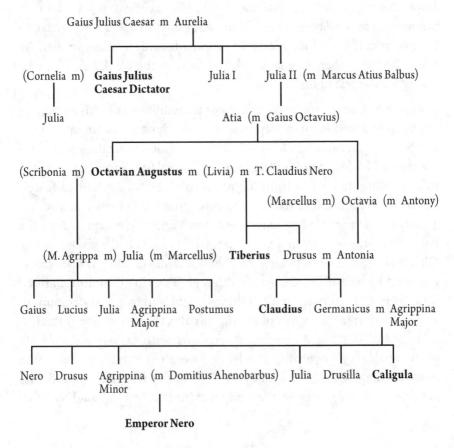

Gaius Julius Caesar  m  Aurelia

(Cornelia  m)  **Gaius Julius Caesar Dictator**     Julia I     Julia II  (m  Marcus Atius Balbus)

Julia     Atia  (m  Gaius Octavius)

(Scribonia  m)  **Octavian Augustus**  m  (Livia)  m  T. Claudius Nero

(Marcellus  m)  Octavia  (m  Antony)

(M. Agrippa  m)  Julia  (m  Marcellus)     **Tiberius**     Drusus  m  Antonia

Gaius     Lucius     Julia     Agrippina Major     Postumus     **Claudius**     Germanicus  m  Agrippina Major

Nero     Drusus     Agrippina Minor  (m  Domitius Ahenobarbus)     Julia     Drusilla     **Caligula**

**Emperor Nero**

Augustus' hopes for creating a patriotic family dynasty capable of ruling his vast holdings were thwarted time and again. He had only the one child, his daughter Julia. He married her to his sister Octavia's son Marcellus, who showed great promise as heir apparent. When Marcellus died very young, depriving Julia of a husband and her father of an heir to power, she was married to Augustus' friend and supporter Marcus Agrippa. Agrippa was a contemporary of her father, and hardly likely to catch a young widow's fancy. However, Julia dutifully presented him with five children. After his death in a few years, Julia found herself betrothed to Tiberius, the disgruntled elder stepson Augustus had acquired through his sensational marriage. Although Tiberius was a talented soldier and a good leader of men, Augustus and Julia learned to detest him, as he made no secret of his grievance concerning his fractured family and his feeling of being underestimated. When Julia's sons and all Augustus' other favored successors died in accidents, disease, or battle, Tiberius became the second Princeps, or Emperor, of Rome. Tiberius' offspring also died before he did, and, ignoring Claudius Nero, the son of his younger brother Drusus, he chose Caligula, the last of Julia's grandsons, as his successor. After Caligula's brief reign and violent death at the hands of the Praetorian Guard in 41 CE, Claudius was made emperor by the Praetorian Guard under foggy circumstances. Though he seems to have suffered some physical disabilities, Claudius ruled surprisingly well, considering the fact that he had been considered, to put it mildly, mentally frail. His greatest achievement was the conquest of Britain, which Augustus and Tiberius had said would be too expensive. Claudius' undoing was his marriage to Agrippina, Caligula's last surviving sister, who cajoled him not only into adopting her son Lucius Domitius Ahenobarbus, but into appointing her son as guardian to Claudius' son Britannicus. Claudius and Britannicus died under suspicious circumstances, and Lucius ascended the throne, adopting, as was his right, the names of his forebears. Thus rose to power the sixteen-year-old now known as Claudius Caesar Drusus Germanicus Nero; he was the great-grandson of Augustus and was to be the last ruler from the Blood of the Caesars.

A glance at Nero's background gives new meaning to the phrase "dysfunctional family." That younger son of Augustus' stolen wife Livia, Nero Claudius Drusus, earned the title Germanicus for victories over the Germans. His son, who had married Augustus' granddaughter Agrippina, was a man of great charm and ability. He had received the title Germanicus when his father did, but he soon earned it in his own right. He won many battles and proved to be an effective soldier and ruler in Germany. When Augustus had been forced by the deaths of his chosen heirs to adopt Tiberius as heir apparent, he had compelled Tiberius to adopt Germanicus the Younger to succeed him. When Tiberius became emperor he removed Germanicus from his friends and loyal provincials in Germany and sent him to Asia Minor, where he died under suspicious circumstances. Germanicus' widow Agrippina made no secret of her belief that Tiberius had engineered her husband's death, and her personal bravery and strength added to her Caesarian heritage made her a dangerous foe. Tiberius disposed of her and her two elder sons, leaving only her daughters and her son Caligula, who succeeded him. Upon Caligula's death one of his sisters, Agrippina the Younger, was determined to regain the throne which she believed her father had been unjustly denied. This evidently was her motivation for cajoling her uncle Claudius into marrying her and adopting her son Nero. Anyone even slightly acquainted with the dour conviction of Germanicus' family that he and therefore they themselves had been cheated of the right to rule could have foreseen a short life for both Claudius and Britannicus. Indeed it seemed that by some grim joke of the gods all the wrong Caesars survived.

When sixteen-year-old Nero came to the throne after the death of Claudius in 54 CE, he was the fortunate recipient of excellent advice in state affairs that helped make his first years noteworthy for excellent administration. He profited not only from the renewed influence of the Roman Senate but also from the wisdom of the Praetorian Prefect Sextus Afranius Burrus and the Stoic philosopher and writer Lucius

Last of the Caesars.

Annaeus Seneca. Seneca, known as Seneca the Younger because his father was also a writer, divided his time between advising state leaders and being exiled or retired. He wrote philosophy, satire, and nine tragedies guaranteed to give anyone a fit of the dismals. These graphically brutal plays, which experts say could never have actually been performed, are said to have inspired some of Shakespeare's grislier efforts.

Agrippina, resenting all these influences and wanting a rulership role for herself, sought to undermine all Nero's advisors. Nero slowly developed an aggressive and cruel personality which led to his executing his mother and many other people whom he believed were plotting against him. Among his victims were Seneca, Seneca's nephew the poet Lucan, and the witty and charming Petronius Arbiter, reputed to be the author of the *Cena Trimalchionis*.

Nero's unbalanced state became more and more obvious; he was even rumored to have started the great fire of 64 CE, which destroyed a great part of Rome, in order to clear the way for his ambitious building projects. He attempted to blame this fire on the Christians, but Rome had seen too many of his excesses, and the Senate ordered him to be flogged to death in 68 CE. To forestall this, he committed suicide by drinking poison on June 9, 68 CE, at the age of 31.

Triumph over Judea deserves a procession and arch.

The chaos following Nero's death brought the Year of Four Emperors. In rapid succession Imperators Galba, Otho, and Vitellius were raised to power and murdered.

When the noise abated a trifle and the blood was mopped up, the dour soldier Titus Flavius Vespasianus, who had just finished subjugating Judea, was Imperator in every sense of the word. The Caesars were no more, and the Flavians had arrived; Vespasian celebrated this event by taking for himself the title "the Caesar."

Vespasian brought peace and stability once more to Rome. His military leadership was outstanding; his economic policies were shrewd but fair. He had none of the appalling vices of the last Caesars, and he worked hard as Imperator; according to Pliny the Elder, the admiral of the Roman fleet who was also an historian, he worked several hours and then slept one, winding up with about four hours' sleep out of twenty-four (Pliny the Younger *Epistulae* 3.5). Rome prospered under Vespasian and his two sons, Titus and Domitian, although anyone whom Domitian, the younger son, considered an enemy was persecuted and destroyed.

After Domitian's unlamented assassination, the Roman world enjoyed two quiet years under the aged Nerva, whose greatest gift to the Empire was his selection of Marcus Ulpius Trajanus as successor. This seasoned soldier and remarkable statesman corrected many of the excesses and inequities of Domitian, expanded the Roman Empire to its largest extent ever, and then settled down to rule his vast domain sensibly and ably. Under his just rule all kinds of activities, including scholarship, thrived.

A learned and honest man.

One of Trajan's able assistants was the writer Pliny the Younger. Pliny, like his idol Cicero, was an orator of grace and polish, but even under so generous an Imperator as Trajan there was little scope for such talents in the political sphere. As a man with an eye to advancing engineering and saving resources, however, Pliny was very valuable, and Trajan sent him to govern the feckless province of Bithynia. Pliny was an accomplished letter writer, and one of his most memorable efforts in this line was written at the request of the historian Tacitus, who wrote to him asking for a firsthand account of the death of Pliny the Elder in the great eruption of Mount Vesuvius in 79 CE. Pliny wrote the requested account, and also one of his own experiences as a young man of seventeen years witnessing and surviving that natural cataclysm.

Publius (or Gaius) Cornelius Tacitus, who was born in the early years of Nero and died in the same year as Trajan (117 CE), was both a Roman senator and historian of the Roman Empire. The surviving portions of his major works, the *Annales* and the *Historiae,* span the history of the Roman Empire from the death of Augustus to the death of Domitian. He also wrote works whose topics varied from oratory to the customs in Germany and Britain. His histories, like the writings of Sallust and other ancient historians, often resemble modern biographies rather than modern histories, as they give the author's personal views and prejudices and include speeches and attitudes composed by the author and credited to historical figures. Tacitus, longing for the values and government of the old Roman Republic, deliberately painted the worst picture he could of the imperial families. He grudgingly admitted that Imperial rule had one advantage: the cessation of the constant civil wars of the Republican era.

In 117 CE Trajan died commanding a Roman army on the eastern edge of the Roman Empire. Trajan's successor, Publius Aelius Traianus Hadrianus, a grandson of Trajan's aunt, was one of Trajan's commanders in the army. Hadrian settled the various eastern questions by battle and diplomacy. He defended, restored, and fortified cities and states; helped the people; and punished criminals. He instituted a professional civil service answerable to the Imperator, which brought about improved finances for both the taxpayer and the government. He ruled carefully and well, often traveling the empire, listening to problems and correcting them. He also managed to find time to indulge his literary and artistic tastes, writing several volumes and overseeing dynamic building projects all over the Empire. In 134 CE Hadrian returned to Rome for the remainder of his life. He had suffered from some time from a painful illness, and, having no children, looked about him for a suitable replacement. In 136 CE he adopted Lucius Verus and bestowed on him the title of Caesar, which hereafter would designate the heir apparent. Verus, who had little time to enjoy his promotion, promptly died. The frustrated Hadrian then chose Aurelius Antoninus, and as a precaution, just in case he too was planning to die, had him adopt two young men, Verus' son and the young Marcus Aurelius.

Although the behavior of emperors had considerably improved in the last several decades, there was plenty in Roman life to call forth the satirists. As we have observed, satire was the one literary form the Romans invented; it started out as a hodgepodge of poetry, prose, and anything else the author could think of, and came to be a poetic form that pointed out, usually with a poisoned dart, the difference between what is and what ought to be. Persius the Stoic in his few and brief poems illuminated sharply the decidedly un-Stoic behavior around him. Martial, while not precisely writing satires, wrote short epigrams impaling various acquaintances. Their names were changed, but evidently that was not enough to prevent their being recognized. After publishing fourteen books of his little epigrams, Martial found it best to go live in Spain. He writes plaintively of his desire for "nights filled with sleep, and days free from lawsuits" (*Epigrammata* 2.90.10).

The creator of the second great vein of Roman satire, however, was Decimus Iunius Iuvenalis, whose sixteen extant poems are simply called the *Saturae*. Ever after brilliant and devastating writings of this type have been known as Juvenalian satire, to distinguish them from the gentler satire of Horace. His history is uncertain. References in the works of Martial indicate that he was an adult in 92 CE, and we know he was alive at least until 127 CE, as that is the year of the last datable reference in the *Saturae*. Pliny the Younger, who was his contemporary, writes to and about many charming and honorable Romans both male and female, but apparently Juvenal never met any of them. Most of his characters were foul and despicable, and those who tried to do well always wound up on the short end of the stick. He was the forerunner of the great playwrights of the twentieth century, whose characters seldom prosper and seldom deserve to do so.

Tacitus was one of the two great historians of this era; the other was Gaius Suetonius Tranquillus. Neither was enamored of the emperors, and both had a gossipy nature, but while Tacitus did occasionally rise to some semblance of impartiality, Suetonius could have been the star reporter for a scandal magazine. Born early in Vespasian's reign, Suetonius was a great friend of Pliny the Younger. Pliny's influence brought Suetonius into favor with Trajan and his successor Hadrian. In 122 CE Hadrian dismissed him from his position as the Emperor's secretary for disrespectful behavior toward the Empress. Except for brief lives and other fragments Suetonius' only extant work is *de Vita Caesarum*, a collective biography of Julius Caesar, Augustus, Tiberius, Caligula, Claudius, Nero, Galba, Otho, Vitellius, Vespasian, Titus, and Domitian. Whether jaundiced because of his dismissal or simply predisposed to believing the worst, Suetonius treasures and expands every bit of scandal ever circulated about the Caesars. As his is the only remaining authority for much of the history of the period, he has perhaps given the world too lurid a picture of them.

Aulus Gellius, a Latin author and grammarian who was born during Hadrian's reign and lived through that of Marcus Aurelius, kept a journal eventually published as *Noctes Atticae*, which he began in long winter nights he spent in Attica, the province around Athens. In this book he recorded conversations, notes on grammar, history, mathematics, and everything else that appealed to his wide-ranging intellect. Of *Noctes Atticae*'s twenty books, we have all but the eighth, and all are valuable for insights into the life of the times and for many excerpts from otherwise lost ancient writings.

Among the many writers of this era, the imaginative, humorous, and irreverent Lucius Apuleius Platonicus, born in North Africa during the reign of Hadrian, stands out, partly because he wrote the only Latin novel that is extant today. Titled the *Metamorphoses*, this work is generally known as *Aureus Asinus*, or *The Golden Ass*, as the hero is early in the novel transformed by magic into a donkey and spends most of the book wandering the world in this guise, learning many amazing things and recounting many tales, the best known of which is the charming tale of Cupid and Psyche.

After the death of Hadrian, the new Imperator, Aurelius Antoninus Pius, whose very nickname is enough to ensure that films will not be made about him, sold the costly Imperial baubles, reduced taxes, and lived at his own expense on his modest estates as much as possible. These facts alone must have been enough to disgust historians hoping to follow the prying ways of Suetonius and Tacitus, but his only real fault was being too much the man of peace; that sort of thing gives opportunists ideas.

The philosopher Imperator Marcus Aurelius, who succeeded Antoninus Pius, had to spend most of his reign dealing with those opportunist ideas and died in a war camp on the northern frontier. (The Pax Romana wandered off into the mist sometime during this era, but, as it stole away quietly, it took people a few years to notice.) Marcus Aurelius saw life clearly and wrote sage advice for everyone. Like Augustus, his **fortuna** did not extend into his personal life, and his clear vision unfortunately stopped short of accurately sizing up his frightful son Commodus.

Philosopher and Emperor.

After the death of Marcus Aurelius, as the second century of our era drew to a close, many aspects of the Roman world were changing, and not for the better. Commodus, son of Marcus Aurelius, longed to be a gladiator, and if the Fates had not indulged their morbid sense of humor he would never have been the son of an emperor. After Marcus Aurelius' death on the northern frontier, Commodus hurried back to Rome to enjoy various athletic delights, some of which were extremely frivolous. While intelligent Imperators like Augustus and Vespasian had shrunk from being hailed as a god and even made jokes about it, the nuttier the rulers were the more they reveled in their supposed deity. Marcus Aurelius may have said that an emperor's purple robe was only sheep hair dyed with the blood of a shellfish, but none of the more unbalanced types believed this. Indeed, Commodus even surpassed Nero and Caligula in his deity complex. He decided that he was the reincarnation of Hercules (remember the athletic delights) and changed his name to Lucius Aelius Aurelius Commodus Augustus Hercules Romanus Exsuperatorius Amazonius Invictus Felix Pius. He then demanded that the names of the twelve months of the year be changed to match his names. Commodus was obviously too busy to bother about such trifles as ruling the world, and he left governing to his unscrupulous favorites, who treated all citizens, high and low, alike—scandalously. The only good thing these paragons did for the people was to murder Commodus.

Next came a longer extended rerun of the Year of the Four Emperors, which came to a screeching halt when Septimius Severus, a great general, became a fair-to-middling, though grim, emperor. The Imperator had indeed become the Emperor, as Severus established a military dictatorship. Although the term Dominus or Lord as an official title of the Emperor only came in use under Diocletian nearly one hundred years later, from the time of Severus the Principate was dead. After Severus' death his murderous son Caracalla was the first of a truly dizzying parade of emperors, and the aging Empire, pausing occasionally to catch a quick breath in the reigns of such rulers as Aurelian and Probus, continued sliding toward destruction until it came to rest against the wall of Diocletian's determination.

# VI. B. DOMINATE ERA OF THE EMPIRE 284–476 CE

Diocletian, a commander of the imperial bodyguard, was chosen Imperator by the army after an assortment of murders thinned down the compe-
tition and his most likely competitor was finished off by a jealous husband.
Until this time Rome had been officially considered a Principate, led by a
first citizen who ruled with the consent and the help of the Senate. Diocletian turned it into a Dominate, ruled by a master or lord, namely himself.
Diocletian did not follow the hospitable open-door policy of Augustus,
Vespasian, and Trajan, having observed that what came through the open
door in his day was likely to be an assassin. He assumed the godlike status
of an Eastern potentate, withdrawing from the people and allowing only
favored ones close enough to kiss the hem of his purple robe.

This new potentate was shrewd, and it did not take him long to see that
a huge empire with the Mediterranean Sea in its middle could hardly be
managed from a single city over on the west side of things. He therefore
divided the Roman Empire into two halves, sensibly called the Eastern
Empire and the Western Empire, and made his friend Maximian, who
was a great soldier and his loyal follower, his co-Emperor for the West.

Diocletian, a natural reorganizer, could clearly see that what Rome
needed was a first-rate office manager. He enthusiastically set about
cleaning out the filing cabinet, which had become crammed with un-
enforced laws, unfinished business, and stray corpses. While setting
things in order he enacted a number of measures in which we see the
beginning of the European nobility and the feudal system, both of which
would make life merry throughout the Middle Ages. During the century
of unrest, the governors of the great Roman provinces, especially those
farthest from Rome, had ruled as potentates and showed a truly imperial taste for throwing their weight around and raising havoc of all sorts.
Diocletian, having split such provinces into several parts, created dukes
and counts to oversee the military while the governors carried on civil
affairs. He felt that a division of power and the resulting squabbles sure

to arise should keep all these folk too busy to do major mischief. He was certainly right about the resulting squabbles: dukes and counts collected more or less loyal knights; swords rattled and banners waved. Foundations were being laid for the Age of Chivalry.

The long-lasting chaos that had given all those governors the illusion that they were absolute rulers had also ruined the countryside. The revenue from lands had fallen, and the various incompetent rulers had responded to the situation by raising taxes. Because of the backbreaking load imposed by money-hungry so-called rulers, people had long been burying their portable assets under the giant oak and abandoning lands because of astronomical tax assessments. Diocletian decreed that henceforth people were bound to remain on the land until taxes were paid. If the land was sold, they were sold with it. For these unfortunate folk the old Latin word for "slave," *servus,* was turning into "serf." While the words are not exactly equivalent, neither represented a very desirable form of existence.

Having reformed such messy matters as a debased coinage, a rebellious army, and obstreperous provinces, Diocletian brought some stability to his world and then appointed two junior colleagues, dutifully called Caesars, to rule subdivisions under himself and Maximian, the two Augusti. These Caesars, Galerius in the East under Diocletian and Constantius in the West under Maximian, married the daughters of the Augusti, carried out assigned wars, and generally did what they were told. Diocletian had warned his co-Augustus that a double abdication was in the master plan, and in 305 CE, after eleven years of reconditioning the aging machinery of the Roman Empire, he threw in the towel and went off to Split to raise cabbages. However this may have affected the cabbage trade, it was rather hard on the Roman Empire, which promptly relapsed into chaos.

Diocletian should have realized that the eleven years of his reign were not nearly long enough to give everybody time to forget the third century pastime of making and murdering emperors. The free-for-all broke out again, and when the plaster stopped falling and the corpses were counted, Constantine, the handsome and talented son of Constantius, had defeated Maximian's son Maxentius at the Milvian Bridge in Rome. He became co-Emperor with Licinius, who had popped up in one of the ruling factions. This arrangement lasted for some ten years, after which the two emperors quarreled. Constantine settled the quarrel with his usual terminal efficiency and became sole ruler of the Roman Empire.

Christianity will serve the empire well.

Constantine wanted to be sole ruler, but he liked the idea of dual capitals. He built a second Rome, complete with an artificial seven hills, at Byzantium on the Bosphorus; he also undertook building in Rome itself. There was rebuilding to be done that was not architectural, however, and for that he cast about him for allies. With his usual innovative insight, he turned an envious eye to the marvelous organization of bishops and priests of the Christian Church, which had been growing and progressing during the long years of turmoil. Organization had been conspicuously lacking in the Roman Empire for many years, and the Christians seemed to have it in abundance. Constantine had had lifelong contact with Christianity; his father Constantius had been a monotheist and his mother Helena, a Balkan innkeeper's daughter who had been the concubine of Constantius, had embraced Christianity with its doctrine that all people are equal. When Constantine was five years old, Constantius upon becoming Caesar had deserted Helena and married Theodora, the daughter of Maximian, by whom he had six children. When Constantine fought his way to imperial power, he raised his mother to Imperial dignity. In her new status she showed no desire for a messy revenge on the various people she might have been expected to resent; her main interest was the advance of her religion. Her forbearing attitude was not shared by her son, who executed various family members, including his eldest son, for mysterious reasons.

Constantine claimed that he had won his battle at the Mulvian Bridge under the Banner of the Cross, and he and Licinus in 313 CE issued the Edict of Milan, which gave favored status to the Christians. He hoped that Christianity would be a unifying influence, but the longed-for unity kept tripping over the Donatist Christians in North Africa and the Arians in the East. At the Council of Nicaea in 325 CE, a majority vote declared that the Arians were mistaken, but they were not terribly impressed. They continued to divide the Christian world, preaching what they thought was right and consigning all who disagreed with them to a warm future in the infernal regions.

Between Christian crises Constantine found time to complete and improve upon the reforms of Diocletian. Between them they ensured the survival of the Roman Empire of the East for another thousand years. The Christian Church, which owed to Constantine its rise from persecuted minority to favored religion, tended to portray him as a saint. Had he actually been a saint, however, both his longevity and his success as an emperor might have been seriously impaired. Having restored the Roman Empire and uplifted the Christian Church, Constantine was baptized on his deathbed and left the Roman Empire to his three sons, Constantine II, Constantius, and Constans.

The power struggles began again, and to make things worse, the Huns, or Scourges of God as they were sometimes called by the more revenge-minded Christians, had plowed through the Goth territory to the north of the Empire in search of elbow-room, plunder, and a little blood sport. The Goths came clamoring to be admitted to the Roman Empire, which like everybody else they wrongly considered impregnable. Sometimes these barbarians were admitted and sometimes not. In either case they wreaked havoc, sometimes even unintentionally.

Ammianus Marcellinus (ca. 330–ca. 395 CE), sometimes called the last Roman historian, recorded events, customs, and curiosities since the times of Tacitus in a massive work entitled *Res Gestae a Fine Cornelii Taciti*. He actually took part in some of the campaigns and events he chronicles, as he served with the Emperor Julian (361–363 CE) in his exploits against the Persians. Only books 15–31 of his work survive, covering the years 353–378 CE. He gives us, among other things, an appalling glimpse of the Huns.

North Africa was an important part of the Roman Empire, and was Roman in culture to an extent hard to imagine today. Roman rule centered around great cities such as Cyrenaica, Carthage, Utica, Cirta, Leptis Magna, and Hippo Regius, and others less well-known. Hippo Regius, on the easternmost Mediterranean edge of modern Algeria, was one of the capitals of the Kingdom of Numidia in Republican Roman times. Under Roman domination it became a center of early Christianity. Its importance was greatly magnified because Aurelius Augustinus (354–430 CE), who as St. Augustine became one of the most influential theologians of Western Christianity, was bishop here from 396 until 430 CE. Under St. Augustine, Hippo rivaled Carthage, whose bishop was widely considered Patriarch of the African Church. St. Augustine's writing, especially *Confessiones* and *De civitate Dei*, were of inestimable importance in the development of Christianity.

The Roman Empire was now forever divided into East and West and the West, due to the fact that the Huns were now sweeping across Europe in that general direction, had the worst of it. In 410 CE Alaric the Visigoth sacked Rome itself, and Rome's reputation for invulnerability took a nasty blow. The Romans hastily called home their far-flung legions, leaving the Province of Britain and other areas to fend for themselves. Neither this nor anything else did much good, and the venerable Empire tottered on toward annihilation.

# VII. REGES ITALIAE 476–526 CE

In 476 CE, after a sickening series of weak Emperors of the West, German soldiers in the Roman army decided that they had played Charades long enough and proclaimed their leader Odoacer *Rex Italiae,* or King of Italy. The last emperor, young Romulus Augustulus, being too much of a nonentity to rate an assassination, was sent to a quiet villa. Then, politely calling in the Roman Senate to ask for the ancient powers conferred on an **imperator**, Odoacer, through the Senate, offered the whole shebang to Zeno the Eastern Emperor, provided that Zeno would appoint Odoacer ruler of the West. Zeno, who had no power to do anything else, named Odoacer *patricius* and **consul**, and the Western Roman Empire toddled off into the sunset.

In 493 CE Odoacer was gathered to his fathers with the assistance of Theodoric the Ostrogoth, who had been invited to oust Odoacer by the crafty Zeno in the sneaky hope that they would fight to the death—of both of them. Theodoric took the entire Ostrogothic nation on this military quest, which should have roused the suspicions of a deep thinker if only there had been one anywhere around. After conquering Odoacer in a couple of battles, Theodoric invited him to a peace parley at Ravenna and, after a hearty and sustaining banquet, murdered him. This settled the two-kings question, and Theodoric settled down to rule Italy.

At last beleaguered Italy got a break. Considering himself the guardian of Roman culture, Theodoric kept the Roman civil service and dutifully named two Romans as consuls each year. He adhered to Roman customs and respected the Eastern Empire. Under his rule Italy received stability and a first-class face-lift, of which it was in desperate need. Like most of his kind he was an Arian Christian, but he extended toleration both to the Trinitarians, who were now known as Catholics, and to the Jews. Both the benefited groups, of course, seemed to think that Theodoric was carrying kindness to excess by extending it to the other group.

As though all that religious tolerance was not enough to give his loyal countrymen heartburn, Theodoric employed various Romans of ancient lineage as high officials. These worthies set about the saving of classical

learning, which in the preced-
ing two centuries of turmoil had
developed a wasting illness that
might well have proved to be terminal. Outstanding among them
was Anicius Manlius Severinus
Boethius (ca. 480–525 CE), often
called the last of the Ancient Romans, who under Theodoric was
**consul** and prime minister (he
was already *patricius* in his own
right). A tireless student, Boethius
as a youth had eagerly absorbed
the best education Rome could
give and then studied at Athens.
His duties at court did not deter
him from setting out to translate
the great works of Greece into

Learning must not die.

Latin, and he produced a translation of Aristotle which was the stan-
dard text on logic for centuries. He wrote commentaries on Cicero,
Euclid, and others (which was fortunate, as most of the Greek texts
were about to take a thousand-year hiatus). Jealous Ostrogoths, who re-
sented Theodoric's favors to Romans, framed Boethius in a plot against
Theodoric's life. Boethius received a death sentence, which in 524 CE
was carried out, but one of his great goals had been achieved—he had
had a great part in preserving classical wisdom for the future. Thanks
to Ostrogothic jealousy he did not live to achieve other goals, such as
translating into Latin all of Plato and all of Aristotle. Perhaps if he had
accomplished this, the Dark Ages might have been less dark and the
Western rebirth might have occurred much earlier. After Boethius was
dead, the aged Theodoric wept for him, but unfortunately this tardy dis-
play of grief was of very little use to classical learning.

# NOTES

**AGNOMEN**

An additional name denoting an achievement or characteristic

**ASSEMBLY OF KINGS**

This description of the Roman Senate is attributed to Cineas in Plutarch's *Pyrrhus*.

**AUGUSTUS**

Majestic; dignified; worthy of honor—title given to Octavian Caesar by the Roman Senate in 27 BCE.

**CENSOR**

One of two Roman magistrates elected every five years to take the census and censor morals. Their term of office was eighteen months, which was time enough to count the people and make plenty of unpopular pronouncements about the failings of the populace. Their name and their functions give us two rather scary modern words—censor and census.

**COGNOMEN**

Surname, family name, sometimes denoting achievement or characteristic—Gaius Julius Caesar's **cognomen** is Caesar.

**CONSUL**

One of the two highest magistrates of the Roman Republic, elected annually to serve for one year. The two consuls were equal in power and commanded the army on alternate days. In case of two enemies attacking at once (which was not unlikely in the Roman Republic's turbulent life), each commanded an army. This novel system virtually guaranteed that Roman wars, even if unsuccessful, were unlikely to be boring.

## CORONA OBSIDIONALIS

Grass crown given for raising a siege, breaking a blockade, or otherwise saving Rome from great peril.

## CURSUS HONORUM

The order of offices sought and held as elective Roman magistracies. In the basic pattern, after military service, a man served as quaestor, praetor, consul and then censor.

## DECEMVIR

One of a commission of ten men.

## EXSILIUM

Banishment from one's city or country.

## FORTUNA

Divine favor or good luck considered necessary for a commander and his followers to succeed.

## IMPERATOR

Title of honor given a victorious Roman general either by acclamation by his troops or by a senatorial decree. Later it became identified with the emperor.

## LATIFUNDIA

Large estates.

## PATER PATRIAE

The father of the country. This honorary phrase, evidently first given to Lucius Junius Brutus after he roused the populace against the Tarquin kings, was applied to various individuals after signal service to Rome.

## PATRICIUS

Originally a member of the aristocratic or senatorial class of Rome. Constantine bestowed the title as an honor for loyal service to the Empire. Theoretically it was needed for a ruler who had the consent of Rome.

## PAX AUGUSTA

The period of peace and stability established by Augustus Caesar.

## PAX ROMANA

The Roman peace, a two-hundred-year period beginning with the *Pax Augusta,* arguably the longest period of peace ever enjoyed by so large a section of the world. The *Pax Romana* was by no means a total absence of war but, according to some rhapsodic poets near its end, a period when a great overseeing government generally sought the welfare of the general populace, allowing many peoples to go about life's business safely under its wide umbrella.

## PONTIFEX MAXIMUS

High priest of the Roman supreme college of priests.

## PRAETORIAN GUARD

When he became Augustus, Octavian recruited the Praetorian Guard from the ranks of the legions throughout the provinces. As his personal bodyguard, it was the only body of armed soldiers permitted south of the Rubicon River, which marked the boundary of Italy proper.

## PRAETOR

Elected official who served as a judge.

## PRAETORIAN PREFECT

Commander of the Praetorian Guard.

## PRINCEPS

First Citizen or Chief, the title that Augustus assumed when he became ruler.

## PROCONSUL

Governor of a province who had served a year as consul of Rome.

## PROPRAETOR

Official appointed to be the chief administrator of a province after serving his term of office as praetor.

## RELEGATION
Banishment to or from a particular place.

## ROMANCE
A genre of literature which slowly came to be written in the language of the common man; that is, in the Romance languages rather than in Latin. It usually dealt characters overwhelmed with feelings and with mysticism in a world very beautiful, but often doomed.

## SATURA
Originally, a dish containing mixed ingredients, later a literary medley of prose and poetry, and finally a literary genre which points out with sharp thrust the difference between what is and what ought to be.

## SECOND PHILIPPIC
Cicero named his fourteen orations against Mark Antony the "Philippics," with deliberate reference to the Athenian orator Demosthenes' speeches which warned the Greeks about Philip of Macedonia's intentions to conquer Greece. Cicero sees Antony as a similar imperial threat to Rome and speaks against him. The Second Philippic was never delivered publicly but was published as a "pamphlet."

## STOIC
A follower of the teachings of Zeno, so named from the Stoa, or porch, where Zeno taught. He taught that men should be free from joy or grief and consider virtue the highest good; this philosophy was very attractive to the Romans, and gained many followers. Some of them followed from quite a distance, however, finding that constant virtue could be a bit trying.

# BIBLIOGRAPHY

Balsdon, J. P. V. D. *Roman Women*. New York: Barnes and Noble Books, 1998.

Butti, K. and J. Perlin. *A Golden Thread*. New York: Litton Educational Publishing, 1980.

De Camp, L. S. *The Ancient Engineers*. New York: Ballentine Books, 1963.

Duff, J. Wight. *A Literary History of Rome from its Origins to the Close of the Golden Age*. London: Ernest Benn, 1963.

Hadas, Moses. *A History of Rome from Its Origins to 529 A.D.* Gloucester, MA: Peter Smith Publisher, Inc., 1986.

Household, H. W. *Rome, Republic and Empire*. London: J. M. Dent & Sons, 1936.

Lewis, Naphtali and Meyer Reinhold. *Roman Civilization*. New York: Harper and Row, 1966.

Mackay, Christopher S. *Ancient Rome: A Military and Political History*. Cambridge: Cambridge University Press, 2007.

Mellor, Ronald. *The Roman Historians*. New York and London: Routledge, 1998.

Sordi, Marta. *The Christians and the Roman Empire*. Beckhenham, Kent: Croom Helm Ltd., 1983.

Ward, Allen, F. M. Heichelheim, and C. A. Yeo. *A History of the Roman People*. Upper Saddle River, NJ: Prentice-Hall, 2002.

Williams, Rose. *Once Upon the Tiber*. Wauconda, IL: Bolchazy-Carducci Publishers, 2007.

# WEBSITE REFERENCES

http://www.thelatinlibrary.com

http://penelope.uchicago.edu/Thayer/E/Roman/home.html

http://www.perseus.tufts.edu

# ANCIENT SOURCES

Cassius Dio. *Roman History*.

Caesar, Julius. *De bello Gallico* (On the Gallic War); *De bello civile* (On the Civil War).

Cicero, Marcus Tullius. *In M. Antonium Oratio Philippica Secunda* (Against Mark Antony, the Second Philippic Oration); *Epistulae* (Letters); *Ad Catilinam* (Against Catiline).

Gellius, Aulus. *Noctes Atticae* (Attic Nights).

Livy. *ab Urbe Condita* (From the Founding of the City).

Martial. *Epigrammata* (Epigrams).

Nepos, Cornelius. *De viris illustribus* (On Famous Men); *De vita Attici* (About the Life of Atticus).

Ovid. *Metamorphoses* (Transformations); *Fasti* (Festivals of the Roman Year); *Tristia* (Songs of Sadness).

Pliny the Elder. *Naturales Historiae* (Natural Histories).

Pliny the Younger. *Epistulae* (Letters).

Plutarch. *Lives of the Great Greeks and Romans*.

Sallust. *De coniuratione Catilinae* (About the Plot of Catiline).

Suetonius. *De vita Caesarum* (Lives of the Caesars).

Tacitus. *Annales* (Annals); *Historiae* (Histories).


(English-only titles are those of authors who wrote in Greek.)

# PHOTOGRAPHY CREDITS

Author Note: The caption for the Julius Caesar bust on p. 38, "Men believe what they want to believe," is a direct quote from Caesar's *De Bello Gallico* 3.18.

# LATIN FOR THE NEW MILLENNIUM
# ENRICHMENT TEXTS

If you liked *From Romulus to Romulus Augustulus: Roman History for the New Millennium*, you're sure to like these other fascinating works also written by Rose Williams.

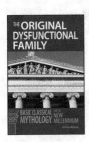

## THE ORIGINAL DYSFUNCTIONAL FAMILY
### *Basic Classical Mythology for the New Millennium*
x + 62 pp. (2008) 6" x 9" Paperback
ISBN 978-0-86516-690-5

A very accessible introduction to classical mythology, *The Original Dysfunctional Family: Basic Classical Mythology for the New Millennium* presents the key stories of the twelve Olympians as well as those of the two gods associated with the fruits of the harvest, Demeter and Dionysus.

## FROM ROME TO REFORMATION
### *Early European History for the New Millennium*
xviii + 102 pp. (2009) 6" x 9" Paperback, ISBN 978-0-86516-718-6

This text provides a comprehensive overview of the medieval and Renaissance periods. While unraveling the multifaceted history of early Europe, Williams gives special attention to the continuity of learning from Rome to the Reformation. In doing so, she traces Rome's impact and Latin's central role in this development.

## THE CLAY-FOOTED SUPERHEROES
### *Mythology Tales for the New Millennium*
x + 70 pp. (2009) 6" x 9" Paperback, ISBN 978-086516-719-3

Greece gave the world its first widely-known superheroes. Rose Williams' engaging style will capture readers' imagination as she brings the achievements, the foibles, and the adventures of the Greek heroes to life. Learn the stories of those individuals who live on in the literary works of the ages.

# HISTORICAL NOVELS

### EXPLORE ROMAN HISTORY THROUGH THE ENGAGING LENS OF HISTORICAL FICTION.
Bolchazy-Carducci Publishers proudly presents the Jaro Tetralogy.

## THE KEY
Benita Kane Jaro
xiv + 210 pp. (2002) Paperback, ISBN 978-0-86516-534-2

**Historical novel on Catullus' life and Rome of the first century BCE.**
The first volume of a dazzling trilogy, *The Key* shows a world on the verge of collapse through the eyes of its greatest and most passionate poet. Gaius Valerius Catullus, the boy from the provinces who became the lover of the most powerful and beautiful married woman in Rome, is dead at twenty-nine. His friend Marcus Caelius

Rufus must search for the meaning of his life in the slums and bloody secret cults, the palaces and law courts of the tottering Roman Republic. Vivid, exciting, carefully researched and beautifully written, *The Key* provides a compelling view of Rome. Jaro neatly interweaves English translations of Catullus' poems into the text of the novel.

## THE DOOR IN THE WALL

Benita Kane Jaro

xiv + 250 pp. (2002) Paperback, ISBN 978-0-86516-533-5

### Political intrigue: a novel on the life of Julius Caesar.

Marcus Caelius Rufus, a young politician, has holed up in a country town in the midst of a bloody and prolonged civil war. Great forces contend for Rome, and Caelius has ties to them all—the charismatic Julius Caesar, his beloved teacher Cicero, the hero Pompey the Great. He must choose sides. To do so, he must reconsider who he is: his childhood and education, his loves and friendships, and, especially, his complex relationship to Caesar, the man who has come to dominate his life. Before he is done, he will discover the shocking truth about Caesar, about Rome, and about himself. This vivid and exciting read is sure to please.

## THE LOCK

Benita Kane Jaro

xxii + 282 pp. (2002) Paperback, ISBN 978-0-86516-535-9

### See Cicero in his milieu: a novel on his life and times.

The major characters and events in the waning Roman Republic are seen from the point of view of Cicero, the greatest orator and finest statesman of ancient Rome. The novel depicts the conflict that led to the collapse of the Republic and Cicero's single-handed struggle which staved off its collapse for 15 years. The principal figures of the age—Julius Caesar, Cicero, Pompey the Great—make their appearance and play out their fateful struggle. The novel deeply rethinks the character of Marcus Tullius Cicero and reassesses his life and work. His warmth and wit, his intelligence, his integrity, and his courage make him a hero for our time as well as his own.

## BETRAY THE NIGHT

Benita Kane Jaro

260 pp. (2009) Paperback, ISBN 978-0-86516-712-4

### The poet of love, the wanton princess, the most powerful man the world has ever seen: a clash of wills and a story of love . . .

In the year 8 AD, at the age of fifty, the most famous poet in Rome, Publius Ovidius Naso, known to us as Ovid, is suddenly exiled by the Emperor Augustus for an unknown reason. His young and beautiful wife Pinaria stays behind to try to salvage something of their lives and to work to bring him home. A woman alone, she is handicapped by the powerlessness of her position. It is not until she leaves behind the world of men to search among the people Rome has forgotten: the women, the slaves, the runaways and temple prostitutes, that she begins to understand what has happened to her life and her husband's, and what the world around her really is.

Historically accurate, deeply researched, and poetically written, *Betray the Night* is a sympathetic reading of the position of women, and a study of the terror of power.

---

Each novel may be read independently or in the tetralogy's sequence (the descriptions are arranged in order). Each novel includes a reader-friendly list of principal characters, a chronology of events, and specially-drawn maps of the Roman Empire and Rome that facilitate your reading.

# LATIN FOR THE NEW MILLENNIUM

Check out *Latin for the New Millennium*—the cutting-edge program for learning Latin and unlocking the wisdom of the ages from the Roman playwrights Terence and Plautus to the revolutionary thought of Copernicus and a heliocentric world.

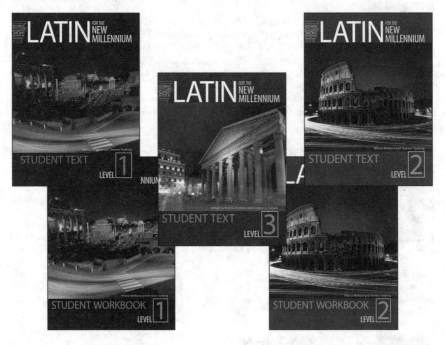

Latin readings are authentic—adaptations from original Latin writings presented chronologically to present the Roman world from its founding to its collapse. Level Two explores the influence of Latin in the medieval and Renaissance epochs. Readings include Bede, Erasmus, Thomas More, and Copernicus.

The culture, daily life, and history of Rome and the early European world are seamlessly interwoven in the text. Special sections on mythology complement the Latin readings. University scholars have written essays connecting today's world with the Roman, medieval, and Renaissance worlds.

*Latin for the New Millennium*, Level 3 transitions students into the unadapted Latin of Caesar, Catullus, Cicero, Vergil, Horace, and Ovid as well as that of Petronius, American colonial John Parke, and Erasmus and his friends. *LNM* 3 introduces students to literary analysis and figures of speech while providing ample grammar review.

## CHECK OUT WWW.LNM.BOLCHAZY.COM

# FOLLOW YOUR FATES

## HIGH INTEREST • INTERACTIVE • ENGAGING • DISCUSSION ELICITING

Our *Follow Your Fates* series offers three exciting adventures as readers from 8 to 80 face the same challenges as heroes Achilles, Odysseus, and Aeneas. Readers make choices but only one path brings success while the others lead to death, defeat, shame, or unrelenting regret.

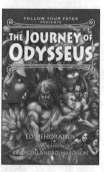

Ed DeHoratius's creative dramatic text is dynamically illustrated by award-winning comic book artist Brian Delandro Hardison.

- *Great for enrichment*
- *Brings the epics even more alive for your students*
- *Perfect for classroom use*

These high-interest books stimulate terrific class discussions. Students come to class eager to share their insights on the choices made as they read. Without realizing it, they're conducting heavy-duty discussion of epic values vs. contemporary values.

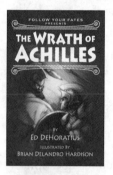

*. . . in forcing the reader to experience these differences between modern day sensibilities and the mores of ancient Greek times, a fresh experiencing of the mythic events begins, in full contrast and comparison.*

– *Midwest Book Review*

*These books provided a chance for the students to travel well-worn paths in an unfamiliar and exciting new format, and as a whole, they gave DeHoratius' books an enthusiastic thumbs-up.*

– Jessica Lahey, Crossroads Academy, Lyme, NH, *PRIMA* Fall 2009

**BOLCHAZY-CARDUCCI PUBLISHERS, INC.**
**WWW.BOLCHAZY.COM**

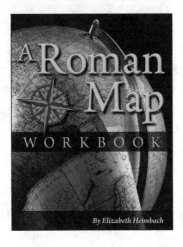
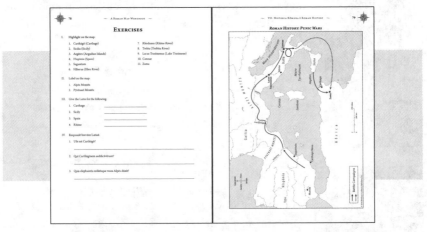